RECONCILIATION:

OR

HOW TO BE SAVED

BY

REV. WILLIAM TAYLOR.

OF THE INDIA MISSION CONFERENCE

AUTHOR OF

"SEVEN YEARS' STREET PREACHING IN SAN FRANCISCO,

"THE MODEL PREACHER,"

"CALIFORNIA LIFE ILLUSTRATED," "ADDRESS TO YOUNG AMERICA," ETC.

I am not ashamed of the Gospel of Christ, for it is the power of God unto salvation.—St. Paul.

Behold, now is the accepted time; behold, now is the day of salvation.—Ibid.

NEW YORK:
PHILLIPS & HUNT.
CINCINNATI:
WALDEN & STOWE.

PREFACE.

THE following pages contain simple appeals to reason and common sense, on the most important subject in the world, addressed directly to any unsaved man, woman, or child in it, who may read them.

The way of Salvation by faith is defined and illustrated in almost every chapter, but the work is extended so as to embrace a broad basis of Gospel doctrines, and an *exposé* of a great variety of hindrances encountered by different classes of sinners in coming to God.

During my recent visitation of the churches in Australia, Tasmania, New Zealand, and Southern Africa the validity of the simple Gospel method of salvation explained in these pages was tested by more than eleven thousand souls, who avowedly sought, and publicly professed to have obtained "peace with God through our Lord Jesus Christ." These were personally examined by ministers of the Gospel, who satisfied themselves, so far as it is possible to learn such facts from the testimony of the parties, of the genuineness of the work of God in each case, and wrote down their names and addresses, and put them under pastoral care.

Among these souls saved were lawyers, doctors, bankers, merchants, mechanics, and persons of all grades down to hundreds of raw heathens from the wilds of Africa. I do not, therefore, send forth this little volume as a hypothetical theory, that may be tried as an experiment, but as the adjustment of God's truth which has been tried successfully by multitudes. It is not a book of sermons, and does not contain a tithe of all that has been proclaimed from the pulpit in connection with the work of

God in Australia and Africa, but it does contain the essential Gospel doctrines, and that practical adjustment and application of them which God the Holy Spirit hath been pleased to employ, and is now successfully using in those countries. I thought at first I would not record these facts, lest it might appear invidious or egotistical, but my "second sober thought" is, that while an ostentatious representation even of the work of God, is a thing to be deprecated, an occasional candid statement of facts, brought out by the testimony of so many credible witnesses, illustrating the mighty work of the Holy Spirit, will do honour to God, and give to poor sinners, struggling in the mazes of doubt, something definite and tangible to guide their weary feet to their loving, waiting Saviour. What a vague inadequate idea we would have had of the great work of the Spirit on that memorable Pentecostal day, if St. Luke had not recorded the fact, "Then they that gladly received his word were baptized; and the same day there were added unto them about three thousand souls."

I have no new discovery to recommend, but a simple explanation and application of the old essential saving doctrines and methods of the Gospel, just such as God hath always blessed in the salvation of sinners, by whomsoever proclaimed, regardless of name, time, or nation. While, therefore, as an humble "ambassador for Christ," I am, in conjunction with my brethren, proclaiming these glad tidings from the pulpit, and daily witnessing the salvation of sinners in this city, I believe that through the prayers of good people, which I earnestly bespeak, and the unction of the Holy Spirit, which I am sure He is waiting to bestow, my little book will travel in a mission of mercy quite beyond the limits of my personal ministry, and the period of my probationary life, and result, instrumentally, in the salvation of very many precious souls.

THE AUTHOR.

LONDON, *February 25th*, 1867.

CONTENTS.

CHAPTER I.

OUR NEED OF SALVATION.

CHAPTER II.

GOD'S PROVISION OF SALVATION.

CHAPTER V.

EFFECTIVE CONDITION OF SALVATION—FAITH.

CHAPTER VI.

OBJECT; NATURAL FUNCTIONS, AND SPIRITUAL GIFT OF FAITH.

CHAPTER VII.

SAVING EXERCISE OF FAITH.

RECONCILIATION;

OR,

HOW TO BE SAVED.

CHAPTER I.

OUR NEED OF SALVATION.

"BE YE RECONCILED TO GOD."

My Dear Friend,—Is it possible, that, like those miserable old heathens in the city of Corinth, you are maintaining a quarrel with God? What hath our heavenly Father done to you, that you should rebel against him, and persistently refuse to be reconciled to him?

Your heart responds secretly, "He brought me into this world without my consent, and now wants to tyrannize over me!"

When the proposition, "Let us make man in our own image, after our likeness; and let them have dominion over the fish of the sea, and over the fowl of the air, and over the cattle, and over all the earth, and over every creeping thing that creepeth upon the earth," was entertained in the councils of the Holy Trinity, where were you, that you could have been consulted?

But, my friend, such a life-charter was not designed for slaves, but for the rulers of this world, second only to the Creator himself. But suppose it were possible that you could be annihilated, and that God should propose to strike you out of being; are you ready for that? "Verily nay!" How sweet is life. How tenaciously we cling to it. If life, with all the disabilities and horrible encumbrances entailed upon it by sin, is so precious to us, what must it have been without these evils, according to the grand ideal of God's "purpose" spanning the brief period of probation, and expanding in a continuous development of human capabilities, in the enjoyment of exhaustless resources of blessedness through the eternal future?

Why should we fall out with God for admitting us "to the race set before us" for such a prize, and for endowing us with powers exactly adapted to the struggle, and a capacity for the "far more exceeding and eternal weight of glory" beyond? Every loyal subject of God, in this world, shall there be exalted to the social status and dignity of "kings and priests unto God."

My dear friend, allow me respectfully to say, that these heart-whispers about the tyranny of God, arise from a vile slander invented by the "father of lies," and by him deeply impressed on the hearts of all "the children of disobedience."

The old "deceiver" commenced to practise his arts upon us in our unsuspecting childhood, and thoroughly indoctrinated us into his creed, the substance of which is as follows:—"God is an austere, hard master. Children are lovely little creatures, full of desires for happiness, and the beautiful world before us is full of pleasures for them, but God means that they shall hate themselves and hate the beautiful things they love so much, and be kept all the time thinking about something they do not want to think about; or be doing something they do not want to do.

"Parents have kind hearts, but forget that they once were children. They have an old superstitious idea of putting old heads on the young shoulders of their children, and of crossing all their little plans for pleasure. Week-days of hard work, and hard lessons, and dry dreary Sundays for committing to memory the catechism, and reading the Psalms of David.

"Ah, my larks, slip away on Sundays and have

some fun, your parents will never know it. A thousand ways of getting pleasure, just try it. Go a-fishing, hunt for birds' nests, ramble in the woods and flowery vales, play marbles, any thing, you cannot miss having a jolly good time. Father and mother did the same things when they were little, and they have got on all right. Every body does it!

"God, and the Bible, and the long prayers are all well enough for old people in affliction who cannot enjoy the pleasures of this life, and for poor sinners when they are going to die.

"It is hard, indeed, if young people so full of life cannot enjoy themselves now, while they are young.

"The Bible says 'The way of transgressors is hard,' but you see it is very easy. It says that 'Life is short,' but you see it is very long. It tells about all sorts of horrible things that shall befall the wicked, but you see that they get on as well as any body, and have a great deal more pleasure than those people who go to meeting every Sunday. It tells about hell in the next world; but if there is any such a place, it is a long way off, and you have plenty of time for the pleasures of life in childhood, then for wealth and honours, and if it should come to the worst, and you find you are not likely to live much longer, why you can repent, and God will forgive you, and you will escape hell, and fare just as well as if you had commenced the service of God in the morning of life." An artful mixture of falsehood and truth, full of the spirit of sedition!

The presumption of Satan is beyond all precedent. He showed Jesus Christ "all the kingdoms of the world, and the glory of them, and saith unto him, All these things will I give Thee, if Thou wilt fall down and worship me." If he had the impudence thus to tempt Him "by whom and for whom all things were made," what would he not engage to give us if we will but renounce our allegiance to God? The lying old bankrupt: he never owned a foot of land in his life; and he never did, and never can, convey one drop of real happiness to any human being. The fact of the matter, my friend, is this: God created us to be happy, and perfectly adjusted His great law of demand and supply to that end. Happiness, immediately or remotely, is the object of universal pursuit, and it is a legitimate object of desire. Every member of the human body, every attribute of the mind, every function of our moral nature, every instinct, appetite and passion, essential to humanity, is, in itself, not only a means of usefulness, but, to us, a source of pleasure. And how perfect are all God's provisions and adaptations of supply, for all these demands! Among these you may reckon the material heavens above us, and the earth, air, and sea, with their teeming resources, animate and inanimate, around and beneath us.

Surely this beautiful, fruitful, harmonious, wisely-adjusted world was not designed as the residence of slaves and rebels, but as the school-grounds for God's own dear children. God's arrangement for our happiness, through all these resources, embraces a wise symmetrical adjustment to secure to us the greatest possible aggregate of happiness for our whole eternity of being. For every instinct, appetite, passion, and power of body and mind there is a legitimate use and appropriate sphere, and time for exercise in harmony with God's will.

Satan's arrangement is to suspend the right exercise of the functions of our moral nature, and as fast as possible to blind, paralyze and destroy our spiritual receptivity; unduly excite and develope sensual appetites and passions; circumscribe our mental vision by the radius of "the things which are seen and temporal;" locate the great end of our being in the present life, and lead us to a reckless misapplication and prostitution of our powers, and a disorganizing, abusive use of God's bounteous provisions.

Satan claims for his arrangement the credit of all the happiness that sinners enjoy in this life. But the fact is, my friend, all the enjoyment any sinner ever had through sinful indulgences, was derived through God-given sources of pleasure. The guilt, remorse, misery, and death involved, are all from Satan and sin. Of his whole stock in trade, he has nothing better to give us. "The" very "wages of sin is death."

I venture to say, my dear friend, you have never been really happy since you became a child of "disobedience," and yielded yourself to the deceitful working of the evil spirit.

A mother, on leaving home for a short visit, said to her two little children, "Now, Peter, I want you, and your little sister Alice, to play here in the yard till I come back. Be good children, and don't go through that gate into the woods, and I'll bring you something good when I return."

"Yes, mamma, we'll be good, and we won't go out into the woods."

After they had played in the yard awhile, Peter

went to the gate, and began to play with the latch, and said, "Sister Alice, I wonder why mamma told us not to go into the woods? I wonder if she thought the bears would catch us? The bears wouldn't catch us, would they, sister Alice?"

"No, I don't think there are any bears out there." Somehow, in playing with the latch, Peter lifted it, and the gate came open ajar, and peeping out he saw a squirrel. "Oh! Alice, here's a squirrel!" and out they both ran after the nimble little animal, till it was hid away among the trees; and then they rambled among sweet flowers with new delights at every discovery, till they came to a small lake, and Peter said, "I wonder if mother thought we would fall into the lake? We won't fall into the lake, will we sister Alice?"

"No, indeed we won't."

When they returned through the gate into the yard, Peter said, "Now Alice, you mustn't tell mamma that we've been out into the woods. She'll be grieved, and may punish us, if she knows we have been out."

"I won't tell her," replied Alice, "but if she asks us, what shall we say?"

"O she'll not think of it," said Peter, "but you

mustn't tell her." Poor boy, he felt a new feeling in his little heart, and a very uncomfortable feeling it was too. The sun did not seem to shine so brightly as before, the flowers in the garden seemed to lose their beauty, the chirping of the birds grated on his ear, and his toys had lost the charm of pleasing. Indeed, he felt so badly, that though he had charged Alice to keep their secret, it "would out." When his mother was preparing him for bed, and had him kneel by her side, and say "Our Father which art in heaven," his voice was so tremulous he could hardly say it.

As soon as his prayer was over, he said, "Mamma, why did you tell us not to go into the woods, did you think the bears would catch us?"

"No, my son, I didn't think anything about the bears."

"Did you think we should fall into the lake?"

"How did you know there was a lake out there, Peter? Have you and Alice been out in the woods?"

"Ah, O yes, mamma, we went out a little piece."

"Ah, Peter, my son, you lost something."

He immediately felt in his pockets for knife, and string, and little toys, and replied, "No, mamma, I haven't lost anything."

"Yes, my son, you've lost a great deal. Now, just think, and see what you've lost."

Peter thought a few moments, and covered his face, and wept.

"What have you lost, Peter?"

"Oh! mamma, I've lost the *happy* out of my heart!"

Ah! my dear friend, you remember when you "lost the happy" out of your heart. Alas! it is gone, and you will never regain it till you are converted, and "become as little children." Then, with a heart full of the reconciling love of God, you may seek your happiness in obedience to his own harmonious adjustments. Then, all the conditions of our probationary state, complicated and painful as they have become by sin, will be laid under contribution in His wise disciplinary "purpose" "to work together for our good." Why will you, my friend, refuse to "be reconciled to God?"

The secret response of your heart is—"His laws are too severe for poor human nature."

Well, my friend, suppose we examine them, and see for ourselves. We have an epitome of God's laws in the decalogue.

The *first* proclaims our great Creator, as God of love, and the only suitor worthy of our supreme confidence, adoration, and love. What a privilege!

The *second* forbids our setting him aside, and substituting some idol in his stead. Surely that command is right. God could not consent to such a debasement of "his offspring."

The *third* prohibits the profane use of His name. Would the British people allow a man to blaspheme the name of her Majesty Queen Victoria?

The *fourth* enjoins six days of labour, and sanctifies a seventh of time—the holy Sabbath—as the proportionate necessary rest-period for man and beast, and for purposes of collective worship. In the institution of human rights to time, is that too much for God to reserve, and "sanctify" for those gracious purposes? The "Sabbath was made for man." The fundamental law of the institution is "good will to man;" and hence, if the statute in any case works injuriously to man, the fundamental law takes the precedence, and in such case suspends the statute; and hence we have a legitimate provision for works of necessity, and works of mercy on the Sabbath. What a merciful institution is the holy Sabbath!

The next six commands are to guard the mutual relationships and rights of the human family against abuse or injury.

The *fifth* command enjoins filial obedience. Are you prepared to say that such a command is not necessary and right?

The *sixth* guards human rights to life. God thus shows his high appreciation of human life. This law is backed by God's ancient penal safeguard—"Whoso sheddeth man's blood, by man shall his blood be shed:" appending the sublime reason for such a penalty, "for in the image of God made he man." In the compensations of Divine providence this penalty is executed by a variety of modes, in wars, and otherwise, besides the legal execution of murderers. The man who dares to outrage this gracious law forfeits his protection. "Murder will out," and God's avenging angel will wait on him, and in due time, rid society of the "bloody and deceitful man."

The *seventh* guards human rights to chastity. God ordained the family relation in Eden, under the sanction of marriage, and guards this sacred institution by the command, "Thou shalt not commit adultery." Could God do less, and do justice to society?

The *eighth* guards human rights to property. I think, as he reserved a seventh of time, so he reserved a tenth of property for the support of His ministers of religion, and for the relief of the poor, providentially leaving, also, a sufficient margin on account of these demands for the exercise of the largest liberality in the way of "free-will offerings." But we have not time to enlarge on that subject to-day.

The *ninth* guards our rights to reputation, than which, next to life and chastity, nothing is so dear to a man. Steal my property, and with mind and muscle left, I can accumulate; rob me of my health, and by proper medical treatment and careful nursing, I may rise and rally, or at worst find an honourable grave in which to rest; but destroy my reputation, and I am ruined. My children for generations would be afraid to trace their genealogy, lest they should run against the nuisance that would expose their shame. How kind of God to guard this sacred interest by the command, "Thou shalt not bear false witness against thy neighbour."

The *tenth* command does not, I think, represent a distinct relationship, like the five preceding, but is designed to cap and bind the whole, by striking at the covetous desire of the heart, which might lead to a violation of any of the nine, especially the five pertaining to our mutual relationships.

You observe, my friend, that in the five guarding human rights, the highest offence in each case only is stated; the tenth mentions the incipient heart-conception of the sin, so that between the highest and the lowest, every form and degree of sin in each case is alike prohibited. They bear equally too upon the whole human family. I am not allowed to kill you, or steal your property; and you are not allowed to kill me, or steal mine; and so with all the rest. Can society dispense with any of these commands? Can it endure even a modification of any of them? To say, for example, that a man may kill a few, but not many, and steal a little, in moderation?

Is it not marvellous that any sane man can believe that the moral law was merely a local Jewish institution, to be abolished by the gospel? The great Teacher says, "I came not to destroy the law, but to fulfil." "Do we make void the law by faith? God forbid," says St. Paul, "nay, we establish the law."

When he speaks of believers not being "under the law, but under grace," in so far as it relates to the moral law, he simply teaches the fact that they are not under the "curse of the law," having been "justified freely," by the grace of God in Christ, and that their obedience now, is not from the legal heart-principle of fear, but the superior principle of that "love" which "is the fulfilling of the law."

Abolish the moral law, and then the majesty and strength of human laws for the protection of society, based on these great fundamental laws of God, are gone. Publish it to the world that God's prohibition of the works of the flesh—"adultery, fornication, uncleanness, lasciviousness, idolatry, witchcraft, hatred, variance, emulations, wrath, strife, seditions, heresies, envying, murders, drunkenness, revilings and such like"—has been repealed, and these diabolical and carnal forces, unrestrained, would utterly desolate the world.

We see, therefore, my friend, that "the law is holy, and the commandment holy, just, and good," and so essential as a legal safeguard to those sacred interests of mankind, as to be of perpetual necessity, and hence of perpetual obligation, "not a jot or tittle to fail," till the material heavens and the earth "shall pass away." Indeed, the great principles of the law are immutable and eternal.

Now, my friend, as it is clearly manifest that God's holy laws furnish you no just grounds of complaint against him, allow me to inquire, whether or not, you have kept the commandments of God? "The man which doeth these things shall live by them."

From your infancy up, has God been the object of your supreme confidence, adoration, and love?

Have you never set him aside, and idolized the creature, instead of worshipping the Creator?

Are you sure you never took the name of God in vain, neither by a profane, nor foolish and needless use of it?

Have you remembered the Sabbath day to keep it holy? You don't remember that you ever went out robbing birds' nests, nor "boat-riding," nor skating, nor any kind of pleasure-seeking excursions on the holy Sabbath? You never did any work on that day, but such as the suffering interests of mankind rendered imperative under the "good will to man" fundamental principle of law, before defined? You never "posted ledger-books," wrote business letters, encouraged unnecessary commerce, or carrying in railways and ships, nor even sympathised with those old speculators we read about, who said "When will the new moon be gone that we may sell corn? and the Sabbath, that we may set forth wheat?"

The mean ingratitude of Sabbath-breaking is

illustrated by the following.—An old man saw some boys playing marbles in the street on the Sabbath day. He did not abuse them and drive them off homeward, but kindly addressed them, saying, "Boys, let me tell you a story." The boys, who are always glad to hear a story, at once stopped their game to hearken.

Having gained their attention, the old man said, "A certain good man had seven pounds, and gave six of them to a poor beggar. The beggar shoved the money down into his pocket, and never said 'thank ye,' but watched his chance, and stole the seventh pound from the good man.

"'Now boys, what do you think of such a fellow as that beggar?'"

The boys all said at once, "that he was the meanest man they ever heard of."

When the old man kindly made the application, the boys blushed, and quietly put up their marbles, and retired to their homes.

My dear friend, have you honoured your father and mother by cheerful obedience, and have you developed such a character, in your relations to God, and mankind, as to afford at once a source of comfort and gladness to your parents, and reflect honour upon them? Alas! how many mothers' hearts are broken, and how many fathers, even before their gray hairs appear, go " down to their graves mourning " under the withering, dishonouring blight cast upon them by their prodigal children.

"Thou shalt not kill." "Don't charge me with that!" I do not mean to, my friend ; but if you are entirely innocent, we can analyze the subject all the more comfortably to ourselves. It is possible to kill without any murderous intent; that is not murder ; but malice aforethought, unexecuted, is murder in the eye of this law. "He that hateth his brother," though he may never have spoken an angry word, much less lifted his hand to strike the fatal blow, " is a murderer."

" Thou shalt not commit adultery." How many genteel-looking men abuse the gifts of God—their money and their talents of usefulness—by plying their deceitful arts to decoy the unsuspecting virgin into the fatal snare, involving her in a life of infamy and misery, more horrible than the pain of many deaths. The laws of God, and the laws of her country, backed by the highest penal sanctions, kindly extended to her their protecting shield, but she trampled it under her feet, and gave up her birthright to the wretch that ruined her. Now, her place in the sacred precincts of her father's household is vacant. Her parents and family are "black with astonishment." They never mention her name; her memory is cast out to "rot." A nameless head-board only, marks the spot where her dishonoured carcase was hid away in the grave.

Many of these, in their turn, lost to virtue and to shame, decoy "the simple ones"—"A young man void of understanding"—"He goeth after her straightway, as an ox goeth to the slaughter, or as a fool to the correction of the stocks; till a dart strike through his liver; as a bird hasteth to the snare, and knoweth not that it is for his life."

My dear friend, I would not charge you with these enormous crimes, but you remember the great Teacher's comment on this law, and its spiritual application to the heart: "He that looketh on a woman to lust after her, is an adulterer," though he may never have spoken to her in his life.

"Thou shalt not steal." Remember, any dishonest appropriation of the property of another, is as really a violation of this law as larceny. The Saviour himself gives it that application: "Defraud not."

My dear friend, I hope you are not guilty of the very common, but most contemptible sin of infracting the laws of truth, in court, or in the social circle, against the reputation of your neighbour.

The tenth command lays "the plummet" and rule to the heart. It is the spirit of man that God is educating for heaven.

Now, my dear friend, are you right sure that you are guiltless? If you have never broken one of these laws in heart or life, you have no need to seek reconciliation with God; but if you have broken any one of them, you are obnoxious to the death-penalty of the law. "The soul that sinneth, it shall die." "Cursed is everyone that continueth not in all things which are written in the law to do them."

One day, when Jesus was returning from a preaching tour east of Jordan, to Jerusalem, "there came one running, and kneeled to him, and asked him, Good Master, what shall I do that I may inherit eternal life?—"Thou knowest the commandments, do not commit adultery, do not kill, do not steal, do not bear false witness, defraud not, honour thy father and mother."

The man was evidently astonished; he thought

he would tell him to do some great thing, and promptly replied " Master, all these have I observed from my youth." He had not killed any body, had never stolen anything, and indeed, had never outraged the claims of society by an outward violation of any of the commandments.

Then Jesus, beholding him, loved him, and said unto him, " One thing thou lackest." Alas ! that was the essential thing. The all-seeing eye of Jesus disclosed the awful fact, that with all his uprightness of character, and ingenuous simplicity, there was such a development of covetous idolatry in his heart, that nothing short of a literal divorce from his riches, would so detach his affections, as to enable him to follow Jesus, love God with all his heart, and attain eternal life, and he said, " Go thy way, sell whatsoever thou hast, and give to the poor, and thou shalt have treasure in heaven ; and come take up thy cross and follow me." He put against his love of riches, the claims of God and his neighbour ; and yet, such was the strength, and blinding effect of his heart-idolatry, that he at once ignored the claims of both God and his neighbour, turned his back on Jesus, and the glories of His kingdom, and went off in the " broad way to destruction."

God cannot accept an outward sham of obedience that is contradicted by the life-principles of the heart.

The man lacked just what we all naturally lack —the heart-principle of obedience, love to God, and our neighbour, without which it is utterly impossible to fulfil the law. We are not only destitute of this essential principle of obedience, but we are naturally corrupt. "The carnal mind is enmity against God, not subject to his law, neither indeed can be." It is not simply at enmity, but "is enmity,"—in its very nature corrupted, and directly antagonistic to God's nature. The natural working and fruits of the "carnal mind" are thus clearly set forth by St. Paul—"And even as they did not like to retain God in their knowledge, God gave them over to a reprobate mind, to do those things which are not convenient: being filled with all unrighteousness, fornication, wickedness, covetousness, maliciousness; full of envy, murder, debate, deceit, malignity; whisperers, backbiters, haters of God, despiteful, proud, boasters, inventors of evil things, disobedient to parents, without understanding, covenant-breakers, without natural affection, implacable, unmerciful: who, knowing the judgment of God, that they which commit such things are worthy of death, not only do the same, but nave pleasure in them that do them." But you are ready to say with the old Pharisees: "That is all true of the heathen, but we have Abraham for our father; we have the oracles of God; we are his enlightened people." Nay, my friend, the inspired apostle has given us, through the light of the Holy Spirit, a true photograph of human nature, as we see from the conclusion he records, "Therefore, thou art inexcusable, O man, whosoever thou art that judgest, for wherein thou judgest another thou condemnest thyself, for thou that judgest doest the same things." That this picture embraces the entire human family in their fallen, unrenewed state, is fully proved by St. Paul's ensuing arguments with the Jew, the conclusion from which is as follows:—"What, then, are we, better than they? No, in no wise; for we have before proved both Jews and Gentiles, that they are all under sin—as it is written, "There is none righteous, no, not one. There is none that understandeth: there is none that seeketh after God. They are all gone out of the way; they are together become unprofitable; there is none that doeth good, no, not one. Their throat is an open sepulchre; with their tongues they have used deceit; the poison of asps is under their lips: Whose mouth is full of cursing and bitterness: Their feet are swift to shed blood: Destruction and misery are in their ways: And the way of peace have they not known: There is no fear of God before their eyes. Now we know that what things soever the law saith, it saith to them who are under the law: that every mouth may be stopped, and all the world may become guilty before God." The Jews were unwilling—as the unsaved portions of the Christian world still are—to admit that St. Paul's former dark picture of human nature embraced them. Then he so adjusted his camera as to put them in the foreground, and the result was the picture just delineated. Look at it. It is not a shade better than the other. The clearer the light the deeper the guilt involved in its rejection. The rejecters of gospel light in Capernaum were immeasurably more guilty than the old heathen of Sodom. The outward manifestation of this deep depravity differs in different nations according to their various modes of education, and is different also in its individual fruits, but the "carnal mind," producing all these various forms of iniquity, is essentially human nature in its fallen and ruined condition.

We will not debate abstractedly the docrine of total depravity. We have to do with palpable demonstrable facts. Through the covenant of mercy in Christ, all infant children commence life in the kingdom of Jesus, and sin is not imputed to them till, coming to years of accountability, they voluntarily "yield themselves servants to sin." Then through the long or short period of their day of grace, they are subjects of the enlightening and awakening power of the Holy Spirit, which has a modifying effect on their lives. Moreover, they may have the most useful gifts, and the most attractive attainments, in the varieties of science and art, poetry, and music, and social virtues. We may add to these, the instinctive parental, filial, and fraternal affections, which we find in great strength in the animal creation as well; but though we gladly, for the honour of humanity, admit these facts, when we come to define our disjointed relationships to God and men, by the "holy" simple standard of justice — the "moral law" — we find ourselves utterly deficient, and hence St. Paul's conclusion from the foregoing argument—"Therefore by the deeds of the law, there shall no flesh be justified in his sight." No man, since the fall of Adam, ever was, or ever can be justified by the deeds of the law, because his very nature is contraband, and he cannot change it any more than "the Ethiopian can change his skin, or the leopard his spots." He may disguise it. He may honourably fulfil the outward duties of life, growing out of all his relations to society. Under the awakening power of God's Holy Spirit, he may do "many things," as did the murderer of John the Baptist, and unlike him, may become as righteous as the Pharisees, who fasted twice a week, paid tithes of all they possessed, and prayed at the corners of the streets by the hour; and thus, so conceal his heart-corruption, and modify its outward manifestation, as not only to deceive others, but effectually and totally deceive himself and go to hell by mistake.

The impossibility of salvation by the law is not because the law is unduly severe, but because our fallen nature is so bad. We have seen that human relationships and rights cannot be maintained by a law less stringent, and if our nature cannot be brought up to the standard of simple justice in our relations to God and men in this life, it surely will not do for the purity of heaven.

What, then, is the use of the law, if we are naturally so weak, and so corrupt as to be utterly unable to keep it?

As a divine rule of simple justice it is so essential as a basis, for the enactment of human laws, and to give authority to their administration for the good of society, that the world, as before shown, cannot dispense with it. It is also used by the Holy Spirit as a moral "straight-edge," by the application of which he convinces us of sin. "By the law is the knowledge of sin." "I had not known sin but by the law; for I had not known lust except the law had said, Thou shalt not covet." St. Paul's quotation of the tenth commandment—the keystone of that grand legal arch, shows, that by "the law" he meant the decalogue. In his illustration of the spiritual end of the law, to make his argument less objectionable, and more forcible, he speaks in the first person singular. He had gone through it all twenty-six years before, in the city of Damascus—"But sin, taking occasion by the commandment wrought in me all manner of concupiscence. For without the law sin was dead." Drifting with the tide of carnal nature we do not feel its force, but throw across it this legal breakwater, and "then the proud waters go over our souls." The frozen snake that lay at our feet is now the boa-constrictor, encircling us in his deadly coil. "For I was alive without the law once:

but when the commandment came, sin revived, and I died, and the commandment which was ordained to life, I found to be unto death." The law was not ordained to destroy people, but to preserve the lives, and great life interests of mankind. But the penal sanctions, which give majesty and force to law, are nevertheless dealt out against the law-breakers. The good system of laws under which we enjoy the protection of life and property, is just the system that is hanging felons every day. The trouble with the sinner in relation to God's laws is that he is on the wrong side. Instead of a loyal subject entitled to the protection of law, he finds that a judgment has been entered against him for high treason against the King, and that he is obnoxious to the death-penalty of the law, already legally dead. "Wherefore the law is holy, and the commandment holy, and just, and good. Was then that which is good made death unto me? God forbid." We never received any damage from the law. Sin did the fatal work. "But sin, that it might appear sin, working death in me by that which is good: that sin by the commandment might become exceeding sinful. For we know that the law is spiritual: but I am carnal, sold under sin. For that which I do, I allow not: for what I would, that do I not: but what I hate that I do. If then I do that which I would not, I consent unto the law that it is good. Now then it is no more I that do it, but sin that dwelleth in me. For I know that in me (that is, in my flesh) dwelleth no good thing: for to will is present with me, but how to perform that which is good I find not. For the good that I would, I do not: but the evil which I would not that I do. Now, if I do that I would not, it is no more I that do it, but sin that dwelleth in me." Here the sinner's judgment and conscience are enlightened by the Holy Spirit. He sees that the law is right, consents to obey it, determines, and earnestly strives to do right, but alas, the carnal forces of his nature are quite overwhelming in their antagonistic risings against God and his laws. "For I delight in the law of God after the inward man: but I see another law in my members, warring against the law of my mind"—God's law, which my mind approves and accepts—"and bringing me into captivity to the law of sin which is in my members."

You understand, my dear friend, the practical workings of that other law—the law of sinful propensities, habits, and associations, stimulated and plied by satanic agency. St. Paul having thus clearly stated the case, proceeds to illustrate it. To appreciate his illustration, you will please to accompany him into an old Roman prison. As you pass down its dark aisles you will hear the groans of poor prisoners from whose hearts hope has taken its last farewell long ago, and you will hear the clanking of their chains till you will shudder, but when you reach the inner prison—the dungeon—your ears will be saluted by the most hideous sounds that ever you heard. They seem to come from a man strangling, and struggling for life. Take a light and look through the heavy iron palisading, and oh! shocking to behold! there's a living man bound to a dead decomposing human body, face to face, and limb to limb; and in his fruitless struggles, which but bring him into more intimate contact with the nauseous, decaying mass of corruption, he cries in utter despair, "Oh! wretched man that I am! who shall deliver me from the body of this death?" Is it not horrible? Yet this is the figure employed by the Holy Spirit, drawn from the custom of Eastern monarchs of thus binding living criminals to the dead decaying bodies of men to pine away in filth and stench till life was gone, to illustrate the hopeless bondage of a sinner in his sins; a justly condemned criminal under the law of God, delivered over to the old jailor, the devil, bound to a body of moral putrefaction, called—"the old man with his deeds." To apply this figure to the personal experience of St. Paul at the period of writing this epistle, when he had been proclaiming liberty to the captives for twenty-six years, is monstrous. How can we on that theory account for the question, "Who shall deliver me?" Saul was delivered from this very state of bondage and pollution about twenty-six years before in Damascus; had been blessed with all those wonderful revelations, to which, in defence of his apostolical character, he alludes in his second Epistle to the Corinthians. He was now the author of his Epistles to the Thessalonians, and his two Epistles to the Church in Corinth, had seen Jesus Christ often, had been up into the third Heaven, had received the gospel itself directly from God, and hence says to the Galatians, "But I certify you brethren, that the gospel which was preached of me is not after man. For I neither received it of man, neither was I taught it, but by the revelation of Jesus Christ." Though his Epistle to the Galatians was written subsequently to his Epistle to the Romans, his preaching the gospel, received directly from God, to the Galatians, was some years before. St. Paul was now on his final farewell tour among the churches he had organized in Asia, Macedonia, and Achaia to commence his new mission in Europe, beginning with Spain, simply touching at Rome on his way, for he says in this epistle, "Whensoever I take my journey into Spain, I will come to you, for I trust to see you in my journey, and to be brought on my way thitherward by you, if first I be somewhat filled with your company. But now I go unto Jerusalem to minister to the saints." Now after all this to find St. Paul in such a predicament as he describes, and crying, "Oh! wretched man that I am! who shall deliver me from the body of this death?"—in utter despair, and knowing not who could deliver him? What have poor sinners to hope from such a gospel as that? Nay my friend, St. Paul personates the awakened sinner, and delineates to the life his wretched condition.

The fact that the unawakened sinner does not feel this dreadful bondage, is no evidence that it is not true, for while he is in body and mind awake, and conscious, he is spiritually asleep—in a state of spiritual death—torpid like the snakes in winter. I read of a traveller in India, who lost his way and took lodgings for the night in a deserted old castle. During the night he had a dreadful dream, thought death in hideous forms was advancing upon him. In his fright he awoke, and oh! horror of horrors! just across his bosom lay a huge *Cobra di Capella.* He could see by the light of the moon-beams shining through a crack in the walls, the gleam of its fiery eyes, and its forked tongue shooting defiance in his face. Poor man, what a discovery! Was his condition any worse now, than before he awoke? Nay, but *now*, he saw it, and felt it.

My dear friend, if you will open your eyes to the light of God's awakening spirit and hearken to his voice, you will find out the facts in your case, and in your struggle to rise you will find that you are not only bound to the body of sin and death, but enclosed in the tightening coil of the old serpent of hell. "Awake thou that sleepest, arise from the dead, and Christ shall give thee light."

Where shall we find a remedy? "Who shall deliver me from this dead body?" Before we proceed to answer this question, let us review the situation of the sinner. 1st, Naturally corrupt.

"The whole head is sick, the whole heart is faint. From the sole of the foot even unto the crown of the head there is no soundness in it; but wounds and bruises and putrefying sores; they have not been closed, neither bound up, neither mollified with ointment." The healing ointment was available in early childhood, but rejected.

2nd. Having "yielded himself a servant to sin" and broken the law ordained for his good, he has become involved in the guilt of high treason against God.

3rd. He is under the death-sentence of the law. "The soul that sinneth it shall die." "He that believeth not is condemned already."

4th. He is in the most abject slavery, "taken captive by the devil at his will," bound by chains of sinful habit stronger than chains of steel, and all the good men in the world and all the angels of heaven added, cannot break a link of those dreadful chains, or remove one foul blot from his conscience. He would fain look to the law for relief, but alas! he is himself an outlaw, obnoxious to its penalties: "the avenger of blood" is on his track, ah! whither "shall he flee for refuge?"

The law can afford us no relief, my friend. It

cannot remove our heart-pollution; cannot impart to us the principle of obedience—"love to God and our neighbour" cannot compromise the principles of righteousness, and exempt us from its penalties; cannot deliver us from the power of sin and Satan. Is there none to save the poor sinner from the deadly coil of the old Cobra of hell? None to deliver from this dreadful slavery of sin?

Yes, my friend. "Thanks be unto God, through our Lord Jesus Christ," I have found deliverance, and you, and every sinner in the world may find deliverance, and victoriously exclaim, in the language of St. Paul, "There is therefore now no condemnation to them which are in Christ Jesus, who walk not after the flesh, but after the Spirit. For the law of the Spirit of life in Christ Jesus hath made me free from the law of sin and death."

CHAPTER II.

GOD'S PROVISION OF SALVATION.

My Dear Friend,—Let us now consider God's propitiatory provision for reconciliation with man, and its application by the Holy Spirit.

"What the law could not do, in that it was weak through the flesh"—the failure of the law was not through any defect in itself, but from the sinful weakness of the flesh—"God sending his own Son in the likeness of sinful flesh, and for sin,"—by a sacrifice for sin—"condemned sin in the flesh, that the righteousness of the law might be fulfilled in us, who walk not after the flesh, but after the Spirit." Whatever the mystery involved in human redemption by the sacrificial offering of God's own Son, and however difficult the accomplishment of this mighty work, the glorious facts are clearly revealed, that the mystery was solved, and the work done by Him "whom God hath set forth to be a propitiation through faith in his blood, to declare his righteousness for the remission of sins that are past, through the forbearance of God." St. John represents this mystery of mysteries under the type of a sealed book. "And I saw a strong angel proclaiming with a loud voice, Who is worthy to open the book, and to loose the seals thereof? And no man in heaven, nor in earth, neither under the earth was able to open the book, neither to look thereon. And I wept much because no man was found worthy to open and to read the book, neither to look thereon. And one of the elders"—an old citizen of heaven, full of seraphic light, and cherubic love and sympathy for sinners—"saith unto me, weep not: Behold the lion of the tribe of Judah hath prevailed to open the book and to loose the seven seals thereof. And they sang a new song, saying, Thou art worthy to take the book and to open the seals thereof: for thou wast slain, and hast redeemed us to God by thy blood out of every kindred, and tongue, and people, and nation; and hast made us unto our God kings and priests."

There are no analogies in nature which will furnish us with a perfect illustration of this Divine work of human redemption.

A familiar historical fact in the life of one of

the Seleucidæ, Kings of Antioch, will imperfectly illustrate the governmental necessity of an atonement for sin. The King's son, the Prince Royal, broke a law of the realm, the penalty of which was that the culprit's eyes should be put out. The King's heart yearned for his son. He could not bear to see him groping his way in total darkness, but what could he do? If he had said, I can't punish my son, I must remit the penalty, and let him go free, his subjects, from the nobles down to the meanest slaves would have said, "Fie! Oh! shame! If it had been a poor man, he would have put out his eyes instantly, but he puts his guilty son above the majesty of law, ordained to protect the lives of millions of more loyal subjects." But the just King, to maintain the majesty of law, and the righteous administration of government, and yet exercise mercy to his rebellious son, submitted to have one of his own eyes put out, and thus saved one eye of his son. No doubt every subject of his kingdom said, Ah, what a dreadful thing is sin against the Government! What a righteous Sovereign! What a gracious father! Our lives and property are safe in his hands, and woe betide the wretch that dare to injure either in violation of law!

If a regiment of his subjects had volunteered to give up their eyes to save the Prince from the penalty of law, the King could not have accepted such a substitute, and if he had done so, the act so far from vindicating the honour and authority of his laws, would have outraged every principle of justice, for society had claims on them that he could not cancel nor ignore; but the King in his independent sovereignty could consent to the personal humiliation and pain of losing his eye, without the infraction of any principle of right, and thus harmonize the administration of justice, and the exercise of mercy.

If any man had been "found in heaven, or in earth," who could have "opened the book"—solved the mystery of human redemption, neither he nor any number of men or angels volunteering to die for the sins of the world, could in justice have been accepted, and could not thereby atone for one sin. But God, the Eternal Word, in his uncreated independent sovereignty, could consent to "lay aside the form of God, and take upon him the form of a servant," "be found in fashion as a man, become obedient unto death, even the death of the cross;" and God, the Eternal Father, could consent so to "commend his love toward us, in that while we were yet sinners Christ might die for us." It is the independent sovereignty and Godhead of Jesus that gives saving virtue to his redeeming work. If he had been a mere creature, even "the first and most exalted of creatures he could not have redeemed" one sinner "from the curse of the law." "Without controversy, great is the mystery of godliness. God was manifest in the flesh, justified in the Spirit, seen of angels, preached unto the Gentiles, believed on in the world, received up into glory."

We have not time to-day, my friend, to go into an elaborate discussion of this great subject, but I wish to call your attention to a few practical facts embraced in it.

First, the dignity, capacity, and immeasurable improvability of humanity. We need no better proof or illustration of it than is furnished by the "story of the cross." If, for example, the Prince of Wales, instead of entering into connubial relations with the beautiful Alexandra, had proposed to marry some beggar girl in London, what would you have said? Thirty millions of stentorian English voices would have responded in one unanimous shout, which would have echoed from the sunny coasts of Australia to the frozen mountains of Greenland, "No!" Why not? Is she not bone of his bone, and flesh of his flesh? "Hath not God made of one blood all nations of men to dwell on all the face of the earth?" Ah! the disparity between his royalty and her beggary, and her utter unfitness to share his royal responsibilities and honours, preclude the possibility of such a union. Yet such was God's appreciation of man, "made in his own image and after his own likeness," that though fallen and degraded, as we have seen, he consented to an indissoluble union of God the eternal Son with humanity, more intimate and perfect than any matrimonal union ever was or can be. When the banns of this union were published in the palace of the Great King, were there any objections? Nay, the enraptured angels became as "a flame of fire" in their burning zeal to accompany the Divine Bridegroom on his mission of mercy, as "ministering spirits to the heirs of salvation." "In the fulness of time" when this union was consummated, a vast company of angels descended to announce the glad tidings to man. One mighty angel outflew all the rest, and as he neared the rocky hills of Bethlehem, in the dead of night while all the busy multitude of men were locked in sleep, he saw "the Shepherds" abiding in the field keeping watch over their flocks. "And, lo! the angel of the Lord came upon them, and the glory of the Lord shone round about them: and they were sore afraid." No doubt they were brave men, and could hold their own with the wild beasts, and the Ishmaelitish robbers, but now they were taken all aback. "And the angel said unto them, Fear not: for, behold, I bring you good tidings of great joy, which shall be to all people. For unto you is born this day in the city of David a Saviour, which is Christ the Lord." The poor men at once saw in their fancy his ensign, royal robes, and train, but nay, "This shall be a sign unto you: ye shall find the babe wrapped in swaddling clothes, lying in a manger." Now the rest of these angelic heralds came sweeping down in their earthward flight. "And suddenly there was with the angel a multitude of the heavenly host, praising God and saying, Glory to God in the highest, and on earth peace, good will to men."

Such, therefore, is the dignity, the intellectual and moral capacity, and immeasurable improvability of man's nature, that God without compromising his own "glory," stoops to take him into his bosom in the bonds of an eternal union.

If man had been a mere machine, or an animal moved only by instinct, or coercive forces, as the horse or mule " whose mouth must be held in with bit and bridle," all the Bible teaching about God's moral laws, and man's accountability; his obedience or disobedience, his fall or restoration, would be utterly out of place. And the idea of God the eternal Word taking upon him the nature of animals—horses, kangaroos, or human animals? The very conception is blasphemous!

Nay, my friend, the being created in "the image and after the likeness" of his Creator, is endowed with powers of intellect, conscience, affections, and will, exactly suited to his probationary situation and ends—a capacity for an intelligent adjustment and loyal maintenance of his right relations to God and society, and an honourable graduation from his educational course on earth to the fruition of eternal blessedness in heaven.

The will, in symmetrical proportion with all the functions of our moral constitution, is nevertheless the grand distinguishing characteristic of it. You cannot rationally conceive the possibility of a moral nature, or moral responsibility, virtue, or vice, nor hence of moral excellence or enjoyment, without a recognition of this fact. The will is the hinge on which all moral responsibility hangs. This fact is so patent to the common sense of mankind, that no matter what their abstract theorizing on the subject may be, in every department of life, in all matters involving moral responsibility, they practically acknowledge and endorse it, and can't ignore it without a repudiation of their own consciousness and common sense.

Man's personal moral agency! Why, every system of law in Christendom is based on a recognition of the fact; every judicial process pertaining to moral action is conducted on a recognition of it; and every decision of every criminal court in the world is issued on a recognition of it. A single example may suffice to illustrate this great fact.

While sojourning in the house of an Hon. M.L.C. in Tasmania, I opened a photographic album on the centre table, and turning it over I called the attention of the good-woman of the house to the *carte de visite* of an interesting-looking face of a young man, and inquired, "Whom does this represent?" She replied, "Ah! that is Mr. ——, the young man who killed our dear son, Henry!" She then gave me a detailed account of the dreadful tragedy that had cast a withering blight over her household, and brought her nearly to the grave. She showed me a letter of condolence received from the "slayer" of her son, and proceeded to tell me what a fine young man he was—the young man who killed her son. "The man-slayer" sent his friend to his account, and hopelessly bereaved one of the very best families in the colony, but had not even forfeited their confidence or friendship. Why? Simply because there was no decree of his will against the young man's life. If it had been in evidence that his will had taken action against his life he would have been hung by the neck and buried in a felon's grave.

Man's moral agency! All the appeals of God to man, his commands, his threatenings, his remonstrances, his reasonings and pleadings, his invitations and promises, assume this as an unquestionable fact of man's consciousness.

The Bible doctrines of man's fall, his condemnation under the law, his corruption, his bondage to Satan as a child of disobedience, the grand work of redemption by Christ for his recovery, his acceptance or rejection of Christ with all the consequences ensuing, all hinge on this fact, and can't be rationally understood or explained without it.

This very fact unlocks the mysterious questions why God's perfected provisions of mercy in Jesus, administered by the Holy Spirit, have not resulted in the salvation of the whole world long ago? and why the great majority of adult mankind are in rebellion against God to-day.

The redemption of the world by Christ, the adequate and available "fountain opened for sin and uncleanness," the offices of the Holy Spirit, and the human agencies employed, are all adjusted to the functions and laws of man's mental and moral constitution.

It is no part of Christ's mission to men to destroy or suspend those functions and laws.

They will stand the ordeal of the final judgment, and its eternal issues for heaven or hell.

The *second* fact I would respectfully submit for your consideration, my friend, is the dreadful antagonism of sin to God's nature and government. If any man in heaven or on earth could have made an adequate sacrificial offering for sin, and provision for man's recovery, surely the eternal Son of God would not have stooped to do the work of a mere man.

If, having undertaken the work, he could have negotiated any arrangement adequate to these ends without laying "aside the form of God, and taking upon him the form of a servant, and becoming obedient unto death, even the death of the cross," surely he would not have taken such pains unnecessarily. It is very evident that nothing short of all he did in the work of human redemption would have accomplished it, and on the other hand, that he did everything necessary on his part for its accomplishment.

The Holy Scriptures, all the way through, are explicit in ascribing the meritorious work of our redemption to the passion and death of Christ: and the triumphant hosts of his redeemed ones in glory, who no longer "see through a glass darkly," but see the King in his beauty, thus address him in a song that wakes all the melody of heaven—"Thou art worthy to take the book, and to open the seals thereof; for thou wast slain, and hast redeemed us to God by thy blood out of every kindred, and tongue, and people, and nation; and hast made us unto our God kings and priests." A kind of divine telescope was put into the hands of St. John, in Patmos, and he took, through the vista of time, the range of the heavenly hills, and put his eye to it, and "beheld and heard," the grand orchestra of glory singing "the new song of redemption." He thought he would number them by squares of ten thousand each, and commenced as they came up within the radius of his field of vision, and says, "the number of them was ten thousand times ten thousand." But after this stupendous calculation, amounting to one hundred millions, finding it was "a multitude which no man could number," he gave it up, by simply adding—"and thousands of thousands: saying with a loud voice, 'Worthy is the Lamb that was slain to receive power, and riches, and wisdom, and strength, and honour, and glory, and blessing;'" and then their swelling melody swept over the battlements of heaven, and the rising millions of the dead in Christ catch the theme, "and every creature which is in heaven, and on the earth, and under the earth, and such as are in the sea, and all that are in them, heard I saying, Blessing, and honour, and glory, and power, be unto him that sitteth upon the throne, and unto the Lamb for ever and ever."

But while the fact is so patent in earth and heaven, that "without shedding of blood is no remission" of sin, and that we "are redeemed with the precious blood of Christ," to speculate on the relative value of his life in this great transaction, or of his resurrection and mediation before the throne of God, is not wise. "Verily he took not upon him the nature of angels, but he took on him the seed of Abraham. Wherefore, in all things it behoved him to be made like unto his brethren, that he might be a merciful and faithful high priest in things pertaining to God, to make reconciliation for the sins of the people. For in that he himself hath suffered, being tempted, he is able to succour them that are tempted." He "was delivered for our offences, and was raised again for our justification. Wherefore he is able to save to the uttermost all that come unto God by him, seeing he ever liveth to make intercession for them." His life, death, resurrection, ascension, and intercessions, are therefore all so many departments of his one grand work. "What God hath joined together let not man put asunder."

It is not wise either to trouble ourselves about the mystery involved in all this. If "the angels desire to look into these things;" and if no "man in heaven or earth was found who could open or read the book of this mystery," why should we be perplexed if we can't work out the problem. It is enough for us to know the fact, that Jesus Christ undertook to solve the mystery, and accomplish the work, and that he succeeded, and cried in his agony on the cross, "It is finished."

The *third* general remark I wish to make on this subject, my friend, is that while "Christ hath redeemed us from the curse of the law, being made a curse for us," he did not abolish the law, nor suspend its claims on our obedience. Nor did he pay our debt in any sense that will exempt us from the necessity of seeking by "repentance towards God, and faith in our Lord Jesus Christ," righteousness and true holiness of heart and life. Christ hath prepared no robes of his own righteousness with which to cover up our iniquity, but "gave himself for us that he might redeem us from all iniquity, and purify unto himself a peculiar people zealous of good works." "By a sacrifice for sin," he "condemned sin in the flesh"—made provision for its entire separation from us "as far as the east is from the west," and hence passed the death-sentence upon it, that it should be destroyed out of our hearts while here in the flesh, and "that the righteousness of the law might be fulfilled in us." Now, whatever may be the grounds of discussion about this righteousness, which we have here no occasion to state, the following facts are clear:—

1. That it is obtained alone through what God

hath done by "sending his own Son in the likeness of sinful flesh," and by the "sacrifice for sin" which he offered, and the condemnation of sin in our flesh, and the quickening purifying gifts of the Holy Spirit procured by Christ.

2. That it is not an outward robe covering, yet not destroying our sins, but a saving power imparted to us, and a purifying work of the Spirit " fulfilled in us."

3. That it is obtained only by those " who walk after the Spirit, and not after the flesh." When under the Spirit's awakening influence we " repent and believe the Gospel," we are " justified freely by his grace." God, through the merits and mediation of Jesus, pronounces the word of pardon. The Holy Spirit communicates this glorious fact to the spirit of the believing penitent, removes the burden of guilt from his soul, erases the death-sentence of the law from his conscience, delivers him " from the power of darkness, and translates him into the kingdom of God's dear Son," and " sheds the love of God abroad in his heart." Such a one is " sealed with the Holy Spirit of promise, which is the earnest of our inheritance until the redemption of the purchased possession," the final consummation of his great salvation—the resurrec-

tion of the body, and glorification of the soul and body in heaven.

The Spirit's seal is a divine certificate of the fact written upon "the fleshy tables of the heart," that the death penalty of the law against him is cancelled, that his sins are all forgiven, that he is brought into righteous and harmonious relations with the moral government of God.

And the love of God, thus shed abroad in his heart, constitutes the principle of obedience, which enables him cheerfully to keep the law—not as the ground of his acceptance with God, but the fruit of the new life he has received by faith in Jesus. By faith he is engrafted "into the true vine, and by faith he abides in him," but the divine sap he thus continually receives manifests itself appropriately in the fruits of righteousness.

"Now, if any man have not the spirit of Christ he is none of his." "If ye love me," saith Jesus, "keep my commandments." St. John gives us the clearest possible teaching on this subject, in exact corroboration of the gospel revealed directly to St. Paul. "Behold what manner of love the Father hath bestowed on us that we should be called the sons of God: therefore the world knoweth us not because it knew him not. Beloved, now are we the sons of God, and it doth not yet appear what we shall be; but we know that when He shall appear we shall be like him; for we shall see him as he is. And every man that hath this hope in him purifieth himself even as He is pure. Whosoever committoth sin transgresseth also the law: for sin is the transgression of the law. And ye know that he was manifested to take away our sins; and in Him is no sin. Whosoever abideth in Him sinneth not: whosoever sinneth hath not seen Him, neither known Him. Little children, let no man deceive you: he that doeth righteousness is righteous, even as he is righteous. He that committeth sin is of the devil; for the devil sinneth from the beginning. For this purpose the Son of God was manifested that he might destroy the works of the devil" out of every believer's heart. "Whosoever is born of God doth not commit sin; for His seed remaineth in him; and he cannot sin because he is born of God." Sin is directly antagonistic to and entirely inconsistent with the divine "seed" of righteousness—the spiritual life imparted to and retained in the believer's soul by abiding faith, and hence to commit sin is utterly inadmissible. "In this the children of God are manifest, and the children of the devil;

whosoever doeth not righteousness is not of God, neither he that loveth not his brother." By this practical personal test, any honest man may find out to which party he belongs. But, my dear friend, we are getting on too fast I fear for your experience. And now, if you please, let us go back and see if we can find out clearly the part the Holy Spirit is to perform in this work.

Who is the Holy Spirit? "The heavens declare the glory of God" and the star-spangled "firmament showeth his handiwork." "Day unto day uttereth speech, and night unto night showeth knowledge" concerning his power and providence in all animate and inanimate creation throughout the world, for "there is no speech nor language where their voice is not heard;" but when we undertake to lay lines on the being and character of God, and define and explain his attributes, we labour under an embarrassment somewhat like that of a ground mole or Norway rat trying to give a geography of the earth. The little animals know enough of the earth for their practical ends of life. So we, from what God hath revealed, may know all that we need to know about Him, for all practical purposes of life and godliness, and will have an eternity beyond for further inquiries.

I would not underrate human powers of research.

Though man in the body is but in his cocoon state, or at best but a crawling silk-maker, his powers of mind in relation to all things legitimately within his sphere of observation and action are wonderful, and but indicate what they will be when he throws off his "mortal coil," and soars aloft to "meet the Lord in the air." But great as are his powers, when he tries to comprehend and define the Being of God, he is like a man trying to bale out the Atlantic Ocean with a bucket. Some learned men have greatly damaged God's cause by speculations on this subject. We can't bale out the ocean, but we can have the free use of it for all the useful purposes to which it is so admirably adapted. Though we can't comprehend the Being, and explain the attributes of God, we may clearly apprehend the great facts God hath revealed concerning himself, his interest in us, and our duty to him.

The unity of design and execution in all God's visible creation, and all his teachings in the Holy Scriptures, proclaim "one God."

The mysterious Trinity of his Being was gradually manifested to the patriarchs and prophets of old, but clearly revealed in "the fulness of time."

The angel of the covenant demonstrated his Divine nature to the patriarchs, and yet the fact that he was a messenger sent by God was an insolvable mystery. Jacob wrestled with him all night, and begged to know his name. "By his strength he had power with God: yea, he had power over the angel, and prevailed: he wept and made supplication unto him: he found him in Bethel, and there he spake with us, even the Lord God of Hosts: the Lord is his memorial."

In this struggle Jacob obtained deliverance from his sins, a new nature and a new name which God only can grant. He found this angel to be God, "the Lord God of Hosts," but his "name," his mysterious personality, distinct from God whose messenger he was, he could not comprehend.

This Divine "Messenger of the Covenant," who was subsequently known as "God manifest in the flesh," is by St. John called the "Word," but more frequently the "Son of God." "In the beginning was the Word," the uncreated eternal Word, for he *was* before created things began. "And the Word was with God"—a clear personal distinction—"and the Word was God"—a perfect unity of Being. "The same was in the beginning with God." "All things were made by him, and without him was not anything made that was made."

The distinguishing titles of God the Father, and God the Son are not to indicate priority or superiority of the first person to the second.

To understand the figures employed in the Holy Scriptures, to convey or illustrate intangible spirit facts, we must ascertain the fact, or particular phase of the subject to be illustrated, and then employ the relevant points, or such portions of the figure as are suited to the purpose of conveying, or illustrating the true meaning of the author or teacher. For example, Christ is called a "lion," a "lamb," a "door," a "way," a "vine," a "shepherd," a "bridegroom." By neglecting the rule I have just stated, how easily any or all these may be rendered ridiculous and even blasphemous, but in their true relation they are all beautifully appropriate and instructive. Even words are but signs of ideas, and must be interpreted by the subject they are employed to represent. I do not mean to say that the titles Father and Son, as applied to the first and second persons of the Holy Trinity are figurative appellations, for I believe the Divine relation thus expressed is essential, and hence eternal, but the human relation of father and son becomes, analogically, the teaching figure to our minds.

You may see God's type dimly foreshadowing the manifestation of these two distinct persons of God, "the Father and the Son," on Mount Moriah. Toiling up the mountain you behold a charming-looking young man with a load of wood on his shoulders; by his side a stern-looking man with a brand of fire and a knife in his hands. You draw near, and hear the young man say, " My Father?" and the other replies, " Here am I, my Son." And he said, " Behold the fire and the wood: but where is the lamb for a burnt offering?" And the father answers, " My son, God will provide himself a lamb for a burnt offering." You see at once that there exists between them the strongest possible mutual confidence and love. You follow them to the summit, and see them together build the altar and arrange the wood; a short conversation ensues in an under tone. You can only catch parts of a sentence now and then, but you soon gather, to your utter astonishment, that the son himself is to be the sacrifice. You see his father's tearful eyes, as he explains to him the will and command of God.

The young man listens and cheerfully assents to it all. He was full twenty-five years old, and could have resisted, or fled away, but without a murmur he consents to be slain and burnt on that altar.

You see them embrace and kiss each other, and can't resist the feeling, when you learn that he is his only son, the embodiment of his own life and love. that the father's is the harder lot. As you see the son yield himself entirely to his father's will, and see the father bind him and lay him on the wood, and draw the knife to slay his son—for a moment the stern moral principle manifested almost absorbs you—All this, simply because God said, " Abraham, take now thy son, thine only son Isaac, whom thou lovest, and get thee into the land of Moriah; and offer him there for a burnt offering upon one of the mountains which I will tell thee of." Now, turn again to the tragic scene, and see in the firmness of the father, and the sweet obedience of the son, the proofs of their perfect loyalty to God; and you know not which most to admire. Compared with each other they are in every respect peers; compared with all the rest of mankind peerless.

High on that mountain, above the ordinary walks of life, rapt in the moral grandeur of this foreshadowing of the sacrificial offering of Christ on Calvary, possibly on the very same spot, the low earthy ideas belonging to the human relations of father and son have no place in your mind.

Is not this sublime spectacle, just as you see it, God's own teaching-type of that wonderful gospel revelation of two distinct Persons of the One

Eternal God, under the title of Father and Son? The relevant points between the type and the antitype, I apprehend are—*first*, perfect oneness of nature; and hence, *second*, perfect oneness of principle and purpose to offer the great sacrifice necessary to the end requiring it; *third*, the love of the Father in giving his Son, equalled only by the love of the Son in laying down his own life. "God so loved the world that he gave his only begotten Son, that whosoever believeth in him should not perish, but have everlasting life." The Son, "for the joy that was set before him" of redeeming the fallen race, voluntarily took the subordinate position of the Holy anointed One, though he was "in the form of God," and "thought it not robbery to be equal with God"—he certainly understood his relation to God. If he was not God's equal, how could he claim to be equal? "But" he "made himself of no reputation, and took upon him the form of a servant, and was made in the likeness of men: and being found in fashion as a man he humbled himself and became obedient unto death, even the death of the cross." We see also the great Shepherd's own statement of this fact—"As the father knoweth me, even so know I the Father: and I lay down my life for the sheep." "Therefore doth my Father love me, because I lay down my life that I might take it again. No man taketh it from me, but I lay it down of myself. I have power to lay it down, and I have power to take it again. This commandment have I received of my Father." We see that while everything he did was an expression of the Father's will, the subordinate position assumed by him as "Our Lord and Saviour Jesus Christ," was as purely the expression of his own will. All acts of worship paid to Christ the crucified, are accepted by the Father as directly addressed to him; for God hath proclaimed, "That at the name of Jesus every knee should bow, of things in heaven, and things in earth, and things under the earth; and that every tongue should confess that Jesus Christ is Lord, to the glory of God the Father." The term "only begotten Son of God" is illustrated by that part of the type which shows the extraordinary love between the Father and the Son—"Take now thy son, thine only son Isaac, whom thou lovest." This expression, "Thine only son," even in the type was used in a higher, holier sense than that of natural generation, for in that sense he was not his only son. When the relation of Christ to his Church is illustrated by the matrimonial figure of the Bridegroom, we of course understand that the relevant points are mutual fidelity, mutual confidence, and mutual love. To carry the analogy further is to render it ridiculous and blasphemous. So with the type on Mount Moriah, we must confine ourselves to the relevant points. A son by natural generation is not only in the likeness and of the same nature of his father, but has also a separate organization of being. But natural generation and its concomitants—as beginning of days with both Father and Son, the separate organization and priority of existence of the father, to say nothing of maternal relationship, are all, in this grand type, as irrelevant and ridiculous, as the idea of a mane and tail to the "Lion of the tribe of Judah." I do not intend to open the old debate about the "Eternal Sonship." I at first adopted, and have always maintained, and still maintain, Mr. Watson's side of the question, but if the illustration of the subject I have just drawn from the Scriptures be correct, it precludes, as irrelevant, most of the points which have constituted the principal grounds of difficulty in the discussion of this subject. God's essential being is indivisible, and hence incommunicable. The title "Son of God," applied to the Messiah, clearly represents to us his distinct personality but perfect oneness with God. The Jews to whom he preached so understood it, and "sought the more to kill him, because he said also that God was his father, making himself equal with God." In the reply of Jesus he said, "As the Father raiseth up the dead and quickeneth them, even so the Son quickeneth whom he will. For the Father judgeth no man, but hath committed all judgment unto the Son; that all men should honour the Son, even as they honour the Father. He that honoureth not the Son, honoureth not the Father which hath sent him,"

The title, "Son of Man," which he so often applied to himself, was also used in an accommodated sense. He was not the son of any man in the sense of natural generation. He was "the Son of Man" in a higher sense; he had taken upon him the nature of man—that "blood" of which "God hath made all nations of men to dwell on all the face of the earth." Now, if this idea of generation was not even pertinent in his human relation, why intrude it into the Sonship, which is to teach us that he is a distinct person, and yet that he utters a grand truth in the highest sense when he says: "I and my Father are one."

The distinct personality of the Holy Spirit, co-equal with the Father and the Son, in the indivisible incommunicable Being of the God-head, and his perfect oneness with the Father and the Son in the projection and execution of the great work of human redemption, and the part that He, as a distinct Person, "proceeding from the Father," was to take in this great work, were all clearly revealed by "God manifest in the flesh," and by the Holy Spirit himself, through the apostles.

"There are three that bear record in heaven: the Father, the Word, and the Holy Ghost; and these three are one." The mystery is too high, too deep, for the grasp of the human mind; but why stumble at that? Every fact in nature involves a mystery that no philosopher can explain or fathom. How the attributes of the human intellect and the functions of his moral nature can be so perfectly joined to a corporeal body, "fearfully and wonderfully made," and constitute a man, is a mystery that we can no more comprehend, than the mystery of the three distinct persons in the essential being of the one Supreme Eternal God. In regard to all material things, we receive facts on the faith of adequate evidence, and let the mystery go. We ask no more for the facts of Divine revelation. The fact of the "Holy Trinity in Unity" is clearly revealed in the Bible, and is distinctly discerned by many intelligent Christians, who personally "know God, and Jesus Christ whom he hath sent, " and who know the Holy Ghost who dwelleth with them."

At the baptismal initiation of Jesus of Nazareth into his priestly office, the distinctive personality of "these three" is clearly manifested. The Sacrament of Baptism was administered alike in the name of the Holy Three.

The apostolic benediction was pronounced alike in the name of the "Father, Son, and Holy Ghost."

The teachings of Jesus, concerning the character and mission of the Holy Ghost, are explicit. He said to his disciples, "If ye love me, keep my commandments. And I will pray the Father, and he shall give you another Comforter;" He was then their Comforter, but was going away. It would be no comfort to send one inferior to himself—"that he may abide with you"—not a few years simply, as he had done, but "that he may abide with you for ever." And who is he? "Even the Spirit of truth; whom the world cannot receive, because it seeth him not, neither knoweth him." God in disguise, God in our midst, to whom his children have access, and with whom they have fellowship, as the disciples had with their incarnate Saviour. The carnal world don't know him, "but ye know him," saith Jesus to all believers, "for he dwelleth with you, and shall be in you." Why should we not know him if he dwells with us?

Again, he said, "These things have I spoken unto you, being yet present with you. But the Comforter, which is the Holy Ghost, whom the Father will send in my name, he shall teach you all things" pertaining to the object of his mission, "and bring all things to your remembrance, whatsoever I have said unto you." You observe, my friend, that this divine Teacher and Comforter is not a mere influence, but as really a distinct person as the Son of God. "He," the personal Holy Spirit, "shall teach you all things," impart all the light and power necessary to salvation and usefulness, "and bring to your remembrance all things whatsoever I have said unto you." The Holy Scriptures are the Spirit's standard of truth, by which we are to discern and test his personal teachings, and "try the spirits whether they be of God." He is, too, our interpreter, to "open our understanding that we may understand the Scriptures." I fear his teaching office is not adequately appreciated even by a large proportion of Christians. When they want light on a mysterious, yet practically important passage in the teachings of Jesus, they will rummage through a whole library of books to find out the opinions of learned men on the subject, when the Holy Teacher, sent by God the Father for that very purpose, is present to give them the very light they need. We may go to the learned biblical critics and commentators to learn geographical, chronological, and historical facts to put us in possession of the local basis of the illustrations of Scripture—places, times, and customs with which the people to whom the lessons of divine truth were first addressed were well acquainted. But whatever may be our reference to text books and collateral sources of information, let us never turn our backs upon our Teacher, but submit all our researches to him, and get his mind on the whole thing. There is no appeal from Him and his clear interpretations of his revealed standard—the Holy Scriptures.

Again, the Saviour said, "Now I go my way to him that sent me, and none of you asketh me, whither goest thou? But because I have said these things unto you, sorrow hath filled your hearts. Nevertheless, I tell you the truth. It is expedient for you that I go away, for if I go not away, the Comforter will not come unto you. But if I depart, I will send him unto you."

In all these teachings of Jesus, the Three distinct persons of the One Supreme God are clearly distinguished from each other. We hence learn, too, that God the Holy Spirit succeeded the incarnate Son of God as the immediate head of his militant church, and the executor of his will for the salvation of the world. The three grand departments of his work, beginning with the world lying in the wicked one, and ending with his final account with mankind in the judgment, are clearly indicated thus: "And when he is come, he will reprove the world of sin, and of righteousness, and of judgment: Of sin, because they believe not on me"—the highest offence only is mentioned, but every subordinate sin is included. "Of righteousness, because I go to my Father and ye see me no more"—his ascension to heaven as our "Advocate with the Father," only mentioned, but embracing all the provisions of his redeeming acts. "Of judgment, because the prince of this world is judged." The final judgment is only mentioned, but the whole administration of justice from first to last of the gospel dispensation is comprehended, beginning with the prince of this world, and embracing all other subjects of government.

In the first of these three departments of the Holy Spirit's work, he is the "spirit of bondage to fear," not binding any sinner, but revealing to him his bondage by sin, and so exciting his fears as to induce him to seek refuge in Christ.

In the second, he is the Spirit of Adoption, the renewing witnessing Spirit, the Comforter, the Sanctifier, the guide of his people through life and death to their heavenly home.

In the third department of his work, as in the first, the Holy Spirit applies the law to the sinner's heart. If he "flee for refuge to lay hold of the hope set before him," well; if not, he will continue to repeat his calls and impart his gracious influences to persuade the sinner to "be reconciled to God," till, by his persistence in "grieving the Holy Spirit of God," his spiritual receptivity is destroyed, and then the Spirit adjudges him a perished soul—a moral nuisance fit only for "Gehenna," "where the worm dieth not, and the fire is not quenched." Ever since the investiture of the Holy Spirit as the immediate Head of the Gospel dispensation, every sin committed is a sin against the Holy Ghost; but the culmination of the sinner's career of rebellion, resulting in the self-destruction of his spiritual susceptibilities, is "the sin against the Holy Ghost," for which there is no forgiveness, because he has destroyed his capability of repentance. Nothing remains now but a "certain fearful looking for of judgment, and fiery indignation which shall devour the adversaries." We see an example of his judicial administration in the case of Ananias and Sapphira. His judicial account with every sinner from the day that he "proceeded from the Father" on his great gospel mission, to the end of the world, will constitute one of the books that will be opened, out of which the dead small and great shall be judged "according to their works;" and that other "book, which is the book of life;" is but the Holy Spirit's roll-book, containing the names of all who walked after him, and accepted through him the free "gift of God, which is eternal life, through Jesus Christ our Lord."

CHAPTER III.

PRELIMINARY CONDITION OF SALVATION—REPENTANCE.

My Dear Friend.—The grace of repentance is Divine, the exercise of it human; when the spirit of "bondage to fear," brings his awakening power to bear upon the conscience of a sinner, revealing to him his relations to the law, his guilt, his heart-corruption, his bondage to Satan, then comes "the tug of war." The light that reveals his depravity excites its opposition. Under the curbing restraints of the law it "works all manner of concupiscence." The voice of the Spirit within, that arouses the sinner to a sense of his danger, wakes up "the strong man armed," who holds him in bondage. Then ensues the struggle before described from St. Paul's letter to the Romans, on the final issue of which depends the sinner's salvation or eternal ruin.

He is now conscious of the working of two mighty forces within him—the attraction of the Holy Spirit drawing him to the Saviour, and the repulsion of carnal enmity and Satanic agency repelling him. "For the flesh lusteth against the Spirit, and the Spirit against the flesh, and these are contrary the one to the other." We have a striking illustration of this collision of the forces of light and darkness in the case of the Gadarene who was possessed of a legion of devils.

Ah, but some persons do not believe in the existence of devils.

Yes, and such persons usually deny the depravity of the human heart as well.

If you please, we will examine this subject for a few moments.

There are certain facts in regard to the existence of which we all agree: there is a great deal in this world that is not right—a vast amount of that hateful thing called sin. You may call it by any other name, but the soul-destroying thing remains the same. Daily papers, periodicals, and books are heavily freighted with its dark details, and yet not a tithe has ever been told. The history of our race is black with deep stains of sin which disgrace humanity and curse the world. I need not stop to give examples. You are quite familiar with them. Jews, Christians, Mohammedans and Buddhists all agree that these facts exist.

Whence do they proceed? Such effects must have an adequate cause. Let any man who thinks himself competent produce a theory that will adequately account for these facts.

If you deny the existence of devils, or their commerce with men, then you have to set down this dreadful catalogue of sins to man's account alone, untempted, unstimulated by any foreign influence whatever. You make man to be as bad purely on his own account as we are accustomed to regard him with all his disabilities, and these satanic agencies added. If that is so, then for the execution of any dark purpose that could be invented in the infernal regions we don't need any other devils; just call man the devil, and we have devils by the million, in the body and out of the body.

So, my friend, you see that theory won't fit the facts.

If you admit the existence of devils, but deny the depravity of human nature, then the question arises—would God abandon his holy, loyal, unoffending subjects to the power of devils, as we find "the world lying in the wicked one?" You know he would not. So that won't work.

There is but one theory that will account for these facts. Though devils and bad men have been trying for six thousand years to explain away these facts, or account for them on some other than the true theory, they can't to this day produce a theory that will stand the test of unprejudiced common sense for five minutes. There is but one theory that will adequately account for these facts, and that is the theory of the Bible, viz:

1st. That human nature is fallen and corrupted by sin; and

2nd. Devils exist and have access to unrenewed hearts, and influence over the feelings and conduct of all who are not saved by Jesus Christ. There is one "prince of the power of the air," emphatically denominated "the devil," but he commands millions of unclean spirits, also called devils.

But you say, Why did God permit Satan to enter the garden of Eden, and why allow him access to our unhappy world?

Our business is to ascertain facts, and adjust

ourselves to them, rather than to push our inquiries into the "whys and wherefores" of God's administration. Nevertheless, it is pertinent to remark—

That as man was placed in Eden on a probationary trial, and as the smallest measure of personal practical holiness necessary to prepare him for his glorified state would enable him to resist all the devils in the universe, it was a matter of but little consequence whether he be tried by devils or some other agency. The same is true of mankind now.

The presence of "the old serpent" in the garden should have operated as a timely gracious warning against the dreadful nature and consequences of sin.

"The angels that kept not their first estate" possibly had nothing to warn them of the danger of sin but the word of God, but our first parents had not only the word of God, but an example. When the serpent impertinently obtruded himself into the company of the woman, and dared to contradict God's facts, her suspicion should have been excited at once, and her wonderful perceptive power would have enabled her not only to detect his diabolical business with her, but also to peer into his nature and define his person. On such a discovery she should have called for the good man of the garden, and said, "Adam, my dear, look at that monster of corruption. That is Lucifer, but he kept not his first estate, and oh! what a wreck! Our gracious Father hath allowed him to come into the garden that we might see in him the dreadful effects of sin. We'll take the timely warning, and never, never sin against God." That should have been the effect then, and that should be the effect now. St. Jude uses this argument, associating the fallen angels and the destruction of the Sodomites, "set forth for an example, suffering the vengeance of eternal fire."

The old fallen spirit with his wily hosts worketh *at* all God's children, and their battles with him are good for the development of their minds and their essential graces, but he "worketh *in* the children of disobedience" only. He can take possession of no souls till they "yield themselves servants to sin." Then he "takes them captive at his will," and no power on earth can deliver them. Very likely the cruel tyranny of Satan is a means of driving more souls to seek deliverance by Christ than could be aroused from an undisturbed carnal sleep without him.

But you say, "I can't object to the argument as to the existence of devils and their power over sinners, but I don't feel his bondage; I have never seen him, nor had anything to do with him."

Not many subjects have the honour of seeing their sovereign. Government is administered through a great variety of subordinate agencies. So Satan rules by a direct "working in the children of disobedience," and also by a great variety of agencies —bad men, bad women, bad boys and girls, bad books, and legions of unclean spirits.

You think you have "nothing to do with him," but if you examine, you will find that he has a great deal to do with you. If you are indeed free, stand up in the dignity of your loyal holy humanity, and say, "I'm free, and I'll demonstrate it to the world by perfect obedience to God's holy will and commandments. I'll never sin again."

Try your hand, my friend, and you will soon find your master.

I once read of a young man who professed to be an atheist, who said he "did not believe in the existence of God or devils." This young man attended a religious service, and two or three

Christians agreed together privately to pray for him. Soon the "Spirit of Truth" shone into his dark mind, and he became convinced that there was a God, and he said, "If there is a God who made me, he must feel an interest in me, and I'll call upon his name, and see if he will communicate anything to me. I went away alone, and kneeled down to pray to God, and there, upon my knees, for the first time in my life, I was convinced that there is a devil."

If you doubt it, my friend, try it.

It is a dreadful thing to be "taken captive by the devil at his will." What is to be done? How can the sinner be emancipated?

Let us turn again to the case of the Gadarene, and we shall not only see the clear illustration of the working of these two antagonistic forces, but see also how deliverance may be obtained. Behold him in an old graveyard overlooking the sea, groping among the tombs. See the scars of the "chains and fetters" with which he had been bound, and which he had "plucked asunder." Hear his hideous howlings of despair! Oh! look at the blood! He is trying to kill himself. He has no knife, but he's "cutting himself with stones." Poor man, we can do nothing for him.

We dare not approach him. Lo! there comes Jesus of Nazareth. He's in the boat: he'll be ashore in a few minutes.

Ho! you man in the tombs there! Look to the sea. There comes Jesus, the man that casts out devils. He's looking! The blood is streaming from the bruises and cuts of the sharp "stones." See his tears. The gracious attraction—desire, faith, and hope—begins to kindle in his bosom.

Hear him exclaiming, "Oh! that's the man that casts out devils! He'll deliver me from these tormentors. I'll go to Jesus."

Here he comes as fast he can run! Clear the track! Down at the feet of Jesus he goes, "and worships him"—cries piteously for help.

Dear me, how he screams! What's that he's saying?

"What have I to do with thee, Jesus, thou Son of the Most High God? I adjure thee by God that thou torment me not."

Do you call that a penitent? You say the man must be drunk, or furiously mad.

Nay; he is just coming to himself. Jesus fully appreciated his case.

What the poor Gadarene expressed so forcibly is

what every sinner, in his approaches to Christ, to a greater or less extent, feels. Here's an important lesson for sinners to learn. Many persons truly awakened by the Spirit, not understanding this complex experience, allow themselves to be duped by the devil, who persuades them that it will never do for them to go to Jesus while their minds are so dark and their hearts are so hard. They must wait till they feel differently.

If the poor man in the tombs had reasoned thus, would he have gone to Jesus? He couldn't get rid of the devils himself. He couldn't get their consent to go to Jesus. The only way for him—and the only way for any poor sinner—was to take himself up under the attraction of God's Spirit, with all his hardness, darkness, and devils, and run to Jesus. The Spirit does not give deliverance away from Christ, but gives the poor sinner the desire, and leads him to Christ.

Under this gracious attraction the Gadarene hearkened, looked, reflected, resolved, ran to Jesus, submitted his case—all desperate as it was—to Jesus and worshipped him. Then the devils came upon him like hounds of hell. They run up every avenue of his heart, try to hold the citadel of his soul, get possession of his feelings and his powers of speech, and cry out against Jesus. But, thank the Lord, they were too late. The poor man had surrendered his soul and his body to his Almighty Deliverer, who, by a word, ejected every devil from his heart.

Whether there were numerically a legion of devils in the man—ten regiments—or devil power equivalent to that much man-power, as we speak of an engine of so many horse-power, it matters not. In either case we see how utterly helpless and hopeless the man was—one defenceless man in the hands of an armed legion—and we see how utterly futile the efforts of any man are to get the devils out of his heart by any performances of his own. All the righteousness of all the Pharisees would not eject a devil, but a word from Jesus will clear out a legion the very moment any poor sinner surrenders himself as did the man in the tombs. See what a sudden and glorious change has been wrought in him! See his beaming countenance. "Joy unspeakable and full of glory" fills his soul. The disciples no doubt having taken him to their boat, and washed him, and given him some clothes, we now see him "sitting clothed and in his right mind."

When Jesus embarked for Capernaum, the poor fellow followed him to the ship, and begged to go along with him. "Howbeit, Jesus suffered him not, but saith unto him, Go home to thy friends, and tell them how great things the Lord hath done for thee." Though left alone amid his old associations, the devils could not get possession of him again unless he again rebelled against God by "yielding himself a servant to sin." The next thing we see of him he is going from town to town in his own country preaching Jesus to the people, "and all men did marvel."

Thousands of examples of this collision of the forces of light and darkness in the penitential struggle of sinners have come under my own observation.

One or two illustrative cases here may suffice.

I was labouring in a series of religious services a few years ago, in Mamaraneck, a suburban town of New York city. Thomas Paine spent a number of years, and finally died, in the neighbourhood of that town. The old people there, to this day, tell of the horrible end of that enemy of God and his Bible. But during his life there he sowed a crop of infidelity that unhappily did not die with him. It had taken such deep root as almost effectually to baffle the efforts of Christian churches there, for nearly half a century, up to the time to which I refer, when

I joined hands with the Rev. Mr. Hollis, the superintendent of that circuit, and we laid siege to the citadel of infidelity and sin. God gave us the victory, and the vales leading to Paine's grave echoed with the shouts of many scores of new-born souls. During that work of God I called one day to see an ex-policeman from New York city—a hardened sinner about seventy years old. Approaching his house, I saw him standing at the gate, and thought him one of the most repulsive looking old men I had ever seen. But for the fact that I had encountered many hard cases before, and had a good brother with me, I should have been intimidated, I fear, and passed on. But I braced up my courage, and prayed that God the Holy Spirit would give me access to his heart. We spoke kindly to him, and he invited us into his house. I approached his heart cautiously, but as directly as I thought I could in safety. As I was conversing with him about the work of God among his neighbours, I saw him feeling in his pocket for a handkerchief to wipe away his tears, and I said to myself, "Thank God, he's a better case than I feared."

At length he said, "I have not been to hear preaching for years till last night, and I've been thinking I am like that wicked old captain you mentioned in your sermon, only I think I am a great deal worse than he was."

He granted us permission to pray with him, and we left him weeping in sorrow for sin.

At the next service I saw the old man in my audience, and during the prayer-meeting, after preaching, I spoke to him, saying, "Father R——, have you any objections to be reconciled to God?"

"No, I can't say that I have; but I can't go forward to that altar."

"Going forward to the altar of prayer won't save you; but as you have been a public sinner against God, it is quite appropriate that you should publicly confess and renounce your sins; and in thus avowing your purpose to seek God, you put yourself in the way of receiving instruction, and of enlisting on your behalf the sympathies and prayers of God's people."

"Well, it may be all right, but I never can go there feeling as I do. I feel wicked. I can scarcely restrain my feelings of anger and contempt at this whole proceeding. I never had any special dislike for the Methodists before, and I can't account for this extraordinary bitterness and hatred I feel against them."

"And yet you feel a strong desire to give your heart to God, and be saved from your sins?"

"O yes, I would give the world, if I had it, to have my sins forgiven."

I then explained to him the nature of this terrible repulsive force that was driving him almost to desperation, and assured him that if he would yield to the attraction of grace, and walk after the Spirit, he would lead him to Jesus, who would cast the devils out and renew his heart.

"Do you think so?" inquired he in surprise.

"Yes, Father R——, I know it. I know it from my own experience, and the testimony of hundreds of persons whom I have seen thus come to Jesus."

"I don't see any use in going there with a heart full of bitterness and cursing: it would be but mockery and not worship. I can't pray, and it's no use to try."

"I don't see any use in your allowing Satan to lead you away from Christ down to hell, when he has sent his Holy Spirit to your heart to show you your guilt and bondage, and lead you to Him who alone can save you. If you can't come to Jesus now, what have you to hope for if you 'do despite to the Spirit of God, and persist in sin?'"

"You seem very confident, but I don't see any possibility of relief, feeling as I do."

"You are not expected to understand how God is to do his saving work. It is enough for you to know the fact that if you will 'come to him' he 'will give you rest.'"

"Well, I know I shall perish if I remain in this state, and though it is against my feelings, and I can't see that it will do me any good, I'll take your word for it, and try to do the best I can." He knelt at the altar of prayer, and tried to repent of his sins, and "believe in the Lord Jesus Christ." But more than half his time there was spent in talking about his hardness of heart, and the impossibility of relief. At the close of the service he was still dark, but felt encouraged to persevere. Next night he was forward again, and in his struggles Satan seemed sometimes almost to "tear him" with rage against Christ. The third night he came forward he was "delivered from the power of darkness, and translated into the kingdom" of Jesus, and publicly told the people what God had done for his soul. He led a new life in the sweetest liberty of the children of God.

I was preaching on this subject one day, at a camp meeting in Canada West, and having explained the bondage of the sinner, and Christ's offer to rescue enslaved souls, I said, "These are demonstrable facts. God's Gospel delineations of human guilt and bondage have their demonstration in your experience, and God's saving facts are demonstrable by every one that will accept his terms of mercy. He does not put any sinner upon a train of metaphysical argumentation to find out the truth, but says—'Prove me and see;' 'Taste and see that the Lord is good;' 'Come' and eat, 'for all things are now ready.'

"Who in this vast assembly will honestly confess his sins, and prove the truth of God's invitation and promise?"

A tall fine-looking man arose and responded "I will." He came forward at once and knelt down and engaged in prayer.

In reply to my enquiries personally, he said, "I have but very little emotional feeling on the subject, but my judgment is convinced, and I have accepted the challenge of the minister to prove the truth for myself, and have made up my mind to 'seek till I find' mercy."

He did not obtain peace with God at that service.

At the evening prayer-meeting of the same day he came promptly forward again, as a seeker, and after the struggle of about an hour, with head up, and countenance radiant with light, he exclaimed, "Bless the Lord, O my soul, and all that is within me bless his holy name!" He had believed and was saved.

Next morning, in presence of a large audience he arose and said, "Friends, I wish in all humility to tell you, for the praise of God, what he has done for my soul. I have always boasted that I was a Briton, a free Briton, but yesterday I found out that I was a poor slave—a slave to that worst of all masters, the devil. Last night, glory be to God, I was emancipated from the slavery of sin and Satan, and this morning I am a free man—a free man in Christ Jesus my Lord; none the less a Briton, but also a fellow-citizen with the saints and of the household of faith. Glory to Jesus!"

Three months afterwards I spent a night in the house of the same man. Found him to be a well-to-do magistrate. He told me that he had been happy in God every day since his conversion at the camp-meeting, except one day he "was in great heaviness through manifold temptations," but cried to God for help, and got a "brighter evidence of God's favour than ever before."

I may just remark further, my friend, that the

gracious influence of the Holy Spirit is adjusted to the laws of our intellectual and moral constitution. He sheds light into our understanding, and imparts awakening power to the conscience, but leaves us free to "walk after the flesh" with its repellant forces, or to "walk after the Spirit," under his attractive drawings.

As a matter of emotional consciousness the repulsive forces may seem much stronger than the attractive, but God is in that apparently feeble desire in the penitent's heart. If you feel it, my friend, don't quench it; let the language of your heart be—

"I'll go to Jesus, though my sins
  Like mountains round me close,
I know his courts, I'll enter in
  Whatever may oppose.

"Prostrate I'll lie before his throne
  And there my sins confess;
I'll tell him I'm a wretch undone
  Without his sovereign grace.

"I can but perish if I go,
  I am resolved to try,
For if I stay away, I know
  I shall for ever die."

As you approach the mercy seat this heaven-wrought desire will well up in your heart stronger and still stronger, till you are enabled to surrender to God, and embrace Christ as your Saviour. The repulsion also will be increasingly stirred in its bitter enmity to God, till Satan is ejected, and sin subdued, by the mighty Jesus you embrace by faith.

CHAPTER IV.

REPENTANCE: CONTINUED.

My dear Friend—Having explained the penitential struggle of the sinner in its relation to carnal and satanic forces, I will now, if you please, try to show you its relation to the law. If you consent to walk after the Spirit, he will lead you first to Mount Sinai. There in the wild wastes of desolation you'll stand till its thunders fill you with awe and terror. Its legal lightnings will play upon your conscience till all your beautiful self-wrought robes of righteousness are utterly consumed.

He will then lead you to the garden of Gethsemane. There you behold the God-man making up his reckoning with the law; you hear him exclaim, "Father, if thou be willing, remove this cup from me: nevertheless not my will, but thine be done." Lo! an angel appears before him—to remove the cup? Nay, he can't touch it, but he is "strengthening him" to endure the heavy curse of the law he hath assumed on our behalf. Now his agonizing cries pierce your inmost soul, while "his sweat as great drops of blood" falls to the ground. There you see the "exceeding sinfulness of sin," and learn to loathe it.

The Spirit next leads you to Calvary, and you hear one say—

> "See the Lord of glory dying,
> See him gasping, hear him crying,
> See his burdened bosom heave!
> Look ye sinner, ye that hung him,
> Look how deep your sins have stung him,
> Dying sinner, look and live!"

You there hear of life, but you see nothing but death. You learn that "Christ hath redeemed us from the curse of the law, being made a curse for us." You feel the dreadful curse of the law, for your own sins close in upon you like the pall of death, and you wonder if you can have life through Him who died for you—when, lo! the legal fire that consumed his sacrificial offering to the death, now blows upon your soul till its carnal cohesion to the world is dissolved, and now "the Spirit's two-edged sword" "pierces even to the dividing asunder of the soul and spirit, and of the joints and marrow," and instead of relief from Calvary, you are thus "crucified with Christ." Now you begin to understand the preaching of John the Baptist, when he says, "and now the axe is laid unto the root of the trees: therefore every tree that bringeth not forth good fruit is hewn down, and cast into the fire"—"He that cometh after me shall baptize you with the Holy Ghost and with fire." You learn that the application of the law of justice, whether to nations or individual sinners, is part of the Spirit's work, "whose fan is in his hand, and he will thoroughly purge his floor, and gather his wheat into the garner, but he will burn up the chaff with unquenchable fire." The words of Jesus then fall on your ears with terrible effect—"Ye shall indeed drink of the cup that I drink of, and be baptized with the baptism that I am baptized with." As the cup could not pass away from Jesus, neither can it pass from us except we drink it. If he had not borne the curse of the law for us, this legal fire would consume us for ever. The baptismal fire of justice which consumed the sacrificial offering of our Great High Priest on the cross, consumes us till "our old man is crucified with him, that the body of sin might be destroyed, that henceforth we should not serve sin." "Therefore we are buried with Christ by baptism unto death."

Christ's death was not to exempt us from our appropriate measure of this fiery baptism with which he was baptized, but to render it a "godly sorrow working repentance to salvation," instead of an "unquenchable fire," consuming the guilty soul for ever; that "sin in the flesh," on which the suffering Christ passed sentence of death, should be destroyed, and the sinner saved, and "that like as Christ was raised up from the dead by the glory of the Father, even so we also should walk in newness of life." Hence St. Paul says again, "I am crucified; nevertheless I live; yet not I, but Christ liveth in me; and the life which I now live in the flesh I live by the faith of the Son of God, who loved me and gave himself for me."

This crucifixion, death, and burial with Christ does not impair the keen consciousness and vigour of the immortal mind of man. It will rise unimpaired above the mortal wreck of the body, and if unsaved, will endure the "second death" for ever unextinguished and inextinguishable.

When a sinner is thus crucified under the law, "and buried with Christ by baptism into death," his tearful eyes are upturned to Mount Zion: and lo! he beholds his risen Jesus in his mediatorial robes on " his holy hill of Zion." Now he hears the voice of the Holy Spirit in his heart, saying, " If thou shalt confess with thy mouth the Lord Jesus, and shalt believe in thine heart that God hath raised him from the dead, thou shalt be saved." In the fact of the resurrection of Jesus he has the demonstrative proof that God hath accepted his " sacrifice of himself " on behalf of sinners; and the great mission of his life and death, both as it relates to the removal of legal difficulties, and the provision of salvation, free and full, for the world, was accomplished. Now the risen Jesus hath become the mediator between God and man, the ever-living Almighty Saviour of all who come unto God by him, " who was delivered for our offences, and was raised again for our justification." While the poor sinner, in utter self-despair, is thus looking to Jesus, " believing in the Lord Jesus Christ," " the Spirit of him that raised up Jesus from the dead," and who will ultimately " quicken the mortal bodies of his saints," suddenly quickens his dead soul, he is " saved;" " reconciled to God" through faith in the crucified and risen Jesus. " Therefore, we are buried with him by baptism into death: that like as Christ was raised up from the dead by the glory of the Father, even so we also should walk in newness of life."

This "baptism of the Spirit and of fire" embraces, in practical effect, the baptismal vows of that Sacramental ordinance; but to appropriate all this as merely a type of the outward application of water is as great a mistake as that the symbols of the Sacrament of the Lord's Supper embody the "real body, blood, and divinity of Christ." The Sacrament of Baptism should not be neglected, but should never be substituted for the essential inward work of the Spirit, in the crucifixion of "the old man with his deeds, and the putting on the new man," of which it is an outward sign or symbol.

Some teachers ignore the doctrine of repentance; but the grace of repentance is one specific end of Christ's mission. "It behoved him to suffer and to rise again, that repentance and remission of sins should be granted to Israel:" and the duty of repentance was the first great burden of the preaching of John the Baptist, of Jesus, and his Apostles. "Jesus came into Galilee preaching the gospel of the kingdom of God, and saying—The time is fulfilled, and the kingdom of

God is at hand; repent ye and believe the Gospel." In St. Paul's farewell address to the elders of Ephesus, at Miletus, he said, in reference to his ministrations among them, "by the space of three years, I kept back nothing that was profitable unto you, but have showed you, and have taught you publicly, and from house to house, testifying both to the Jews, and also to the Greeks, repentance toward God, and faith toward our Lord Jesus Christ."

But, my dear friend, I would have you to understand, distinctly, that in all this fiery ordeal of repentance we have described, there is nothing meritorious on our part. "Though I give all my goods to feed the poor, and though I give my body to be burned, and have not charity," or the renewing love of God in my heart, which I obtain through faith in Jesus, "it profiteth me nothing." There is but "one sacrifice for sins."

The practical end or object of repentance is simply unreserved submission to God's will, a consent that he take out of our hearts everything opposed to his will, though as dear to our carnal nature as a "right eye or right hand," and freely accept his will as the rule of our lives. His will is perfectly right, and perfectly consistent with our best interests here and hereafter for ever, embracing every legitimate relation, duty, and privilege of life. He does not require any soul to give up something for nothing, but to renounce all sin, because it is rubbish and death, to make room for the "gift of God, which is eternal life through Jesus Christ our Lord." If "for the kingdom of God" a soul is called upon to make a sacrifice of that which is legitimate in itself and dear to him, God provides the most munificent indemnification, "even an hundred-fold in the present time, and in the world to come everlasting life."

It is a great shame to humanity that the Holy Spirit finds it necessary to lead us through the baptism of fire before we will submit to God's will; but such is the fact. Just at that point of submission—whether with many tears, or no tears at all—whether by ten years' or ten minutes' repentance, it matters not as to time—the sooner the better—the sinner may "believe," and be "saved."

Saul of Tarsus endured this crucifixion on his way to Damascus, and was buried by this baptism into death for three days, till his prejudice, pride, self-righteousness, and all things in which he gloried were consumed, and from the depths of utter self-despair, under the teaching of Ananias, he accepted in Jesus Christ "the power of God unto salvation." Upwards of thirty years afterwards, St. Paul, referring to this momentous period of his life, speaking of the things whereof he gloried before, said—"But what things were gain to me, those I counted loss for Christ. Yea, doubtless, and I count all things but loss for the excellency of the knowledge of Christ Jesus my Lord; for whom I have suffered the loss of all things, and do count them but dung, that I may win Christ, and be found in him, not having mine own righteousness, which is of the law, but that which is through the faith of Christ, the righteousness which is of God by faith." The three thousand souls saved on the very day the Holy Spirit descended and commenced his great work of saving the world, reached this essential point of submission under the preaching of a single sermon. "When they heard this"—the gospel of Jesus—"they were pricked in their heart, and said unto Peter and the rest of the apostles, Men and brethren, what shall we do?" Wonderful as was this power of the Holy Spirit, it was not coercive, but perfectly adjusted to the laws of their intellectual and moral constitution. They were enlightened and awakened, and cried out in the bitterness of penitential sorrow, "Men and brethren, what shall we do?" Suitable instructions were addressed to their understanding and heart, and three thousand of them "gladly received the Word" which was the basis and medium of their faith; thus repenting, they believed; and receiving the Holy Spirit in his regenerating power, were baptized, and thus publicly admitted into the visible church of Christ, and all in the space of a few hours. So under St. Paul's first sermon in Antioch in Pisidia, "when the congregation was broken up, many of the Jews and religious proselytes followed Paul and Barnabas; who speaking to them persuaded them to continue in the grace of God." They must have received the grace of God, or they could not be persuaded to continue in it.

"And it came to pass in Iconium, that they went both together into the synagogue of the Jews, and so spake that a great multitude both of Jews and also of the Greeks believed."

So also in Philippi multitudes were saved in a very short time. There was Lydia, "whose heart the Lord opened, that she attended unto the things which were spoken of Paul." She not only heard them, but "attended unto the things"—yielded prompt obedience, and the result was she was saved and baptized that day, and took the preachers home with her to abide.

So the jailor, when by a combination of providential circumstances, the Holy Spirit "reproved him of sin," and revealed to him his bondage and condemnation, he cried out, "Sirs, what must I do to be saved?" Did St. Paul tell him to learn to read the Scriptures, treat the prisoners better, and lead a new life? Nay, he knew his heart was corrupt, and that he never could improve his state, nor could he by any means remove the death sentence of the law from himself, but he saw that he had reached this essential point of submission, and hence said to him, "believe on the Lord Jesus Christ, and thou shalt be saved, and thy house." He did believe, "and was baptized, he and all his, straightway."

So also under St. Paul's sermon on "Mars' Hill certain men clave unto him, and believed: among whom was Dionysius the Areopagite—one of the judges of that celebrated court—and a woman named Damaris, and others with them." And so in Corinth, and wherever they went "the Word of the Lord had free course and was glorified" in the salvation of sinners.

When God's ministers and people seek the prophetic unction of the Holy Spirit and clearly witness to "the truth as it is in Jesus," St. Paul tells us plainly the effect upon sinners. "If all prophesy, and there come in one that believeth not, or one unlearned, he is convinced of all, he is judged of all: and thus are the secrets of his heart made manifest: and so falling down on his face he will worship God, and report that God is in you of a truth." Here is the case of "one unlearned"—a poor heathen who never heard the gospel before, "or one that believeth not"—though he had heard it, he didn't believe it,—under the teaching power of the combined testimony of Jesus' witnesses, convinced of the truth of their statements, and as a consequence "is judged" through the application of the law by the reproving Spirit of God, "and so falling down on his face"—then and there, "he worships God," and finds salvation, so as to be able as a personal witness "to report that God is in you of a truth." This is not given as an isolated case, but as an illustrative example of a rule that is applicable under the conditions specified by St. Paul, to every age and nation "till every knee shall bow and every tongue confess that Jesus Christ is Lord to the glory of God the Father."

But, my dear Friend, however long or short the

penitential struggle of the sinner, this point of submission must be reached before he can in the gospel saving sense, "believe on the Lord Jesus Christ."

Jesus did not come to save us in our sins, but from our sins; not against our will, but with our free consent; to receive him, therefore, as a Saviour from sin, implies in the nature of the case our hearty consent to a divorce from sin. Yet such is our carnal capriciousness, blindness, stubbornness and pride that we will not submit to this simple principle of righteousness till we are slain by the Spirit's legal sword.

A man in Melbourne was seeking pardon for days, but could get no relief. Many of his friends wondered why, and they seemed almost disposed to charge God with "slackness concerning his promise."

Finally he called on me privately and said, "I know the difficulty in my case. Some years ago my wages were not equal to my imaginary wants, and I ventured occasionally to take a shilling from my master's money. A great deal of cash passed through my hands, and I knew he never would know it, and thought it a small matter. I took in all about twenty pounds. When I heard you preach the other night about restitution I saw at once that I never could be saved till I 'gave again that I had robbed.' I will make restitution; I am thankful to say I am able to do it, and will pay back thirty pounds for the twenty I have taken, but I want to know if I will have to confess the theft to my master. I am still employed by the same man, and he has entire confidence in me, and I can return the money as I took it, without his knowing anything about it." He then explained to me some peculiar facts in regard to his family and business relationships.

I replied that under ordinary circumstances, and in all cases when the injured party had knowledge of the fact, a confession was an essential part of the business, but I believed there were cases in which a confession of that sort might do serious damage, and when no principle of justice required it, I believed the restitution without the confession would meet the demands of righteousness. I thought under all the circumstances of his case the restitution without the confession would be sufficient. He did accordingly, and found peace with God that day.

But another man in Victoria who had dishonestly appropriated one hundred and fifty pounds of his neighbour's money, and slandered and abused him besides, could find no relief at our altars of prayer, till he had not only arranged the matter of restitution, but made confession, and, so far as he could, repaired the damage he had done to the reputation of his neighbour. He wrote him a letter, asking his pardon, and requesting the injured man, who forgave him freely, to make any use of it he thought proper for the reparation of the injury he had received by "false witness."

A young man in Cornwall came out avowedly as a seeker of salvation, and wept and prayed aloud for hours, but could get no comfort.

A friend of mine, knowing something of his home relationships, said to him, "Christopher, is it all right with you at home; are you on good terms with your mother?"

"No, I haven't spoken to her for three months!"

"Now, Christopher, you must 'leave thy gift at the altar, first go and be reconciled to thy mother, and then come and offer thy gift.' If it was possible for you to weep your eyes out, you could not find peace with God while you cherish an unforgiving spirit to your mother. Jesus says 'Forgive if ye have aught against any, that your Father also which is in heaven may forgive you; for if ye do not in your hearts forgive men their trespasses, neither will your Father which is in heaven forgive you your trespasses.' If you will go and be reconciled to your mother, I will go with you if you wish." Christopher consented, and when they got to the young man's home, which was near the chapel, the father met them at the door, and my friend said to him, "Here's Christopher; he has been seeking salvation at the meeting, and can't find it till he is first reconciled to his mother, and he has come for that purpose."

"Come in, my son," said the father, "come in." The mother was called; the mother and son embraced each other and wept, and he asked her pardon, he then dropped on his knees, submitted, believed in Jesus, and found peace with God straightway.

I mention these cases simply as illustrative examples of a vast variety of hindrances which often prevent sinners from submitting themselves to God.

Any dislodged idol in the heart, any cherished bosom sin, any mental reservations whatever, will preclude the fact of your submission, and hence preclude the possibility of believing unto salvation.

Seeking merely as an experiment will not do either.

There must be an honest confession, and renunciation of sin, and an unreserved consecration of heart and life to God for time and for eternity.

But you say, "How do you reconcile all this doing, especially in the matter of restitution, with the doctrine of present salvation by faith?"

God is very kind, and will do every thing consistent with the law of righteousness to meet the peculiarities of every case. Sin is a thing of the heart; repentance, believing, and holiness are things of the heart. This baptismal ordeal we have described has mainly to do with the heart. To be effective it must lead the sinner to give up all unrighteous heart-principles, and adopt right ones. Where this is the case it will manifest itself in outward "fruits meet for repentance." In the matter of restitution, for example, the moment the sinner submits, and believes, he will obtain pardon; but the overt act of restitution may be delayed till he is able to fulfil it; and if he has not the ability, and cannot acquire it, his inability will not vitiate the righteous principles of his heart, or work a forfeiture of the saving mercy of God. For example, there was the case of the little publican Zaccheus. Concealed in the boughs of a "sycamore tree" on the road from Jericho to Jerusalem. He thought to get a good look at the great Teacher without being observed; but as Jesus came underneath, and the curious publican was straining his eyes to discern some wonderful attractions in his person, he stopped—ah! a rare opportunity for seeing him—and looking up, said "*Z*accheus!"—dear me, didn't it strike him—"Oh! this is the all-seeing, all-knowing One. He knows my name, my heart, he is Messiah!"—"Zaccheus, make haste and come down, for I must abide at thy house." And he made haste, and came down, and received him joyfully, and in the exuberance of his penitential honesty he "stood and said unto the Lord—Behold, Lord, the half of my goods I give to the poor"—restitution to God on behalf of his poor—"and if I have taken any thing from any man, by false accusation," making false tax returns and pocketing the difference—"I restore him fourfold." "And Jesus said unto him, This day is salvation come to this house; for the Son of Man is come to seek and to save that which was lost." Zaccheus had not as yet paid a farthing, but Jesus knew his heart, and gave him salvation on his prompt heart obedience and faith. This baptism of fire, as before stated, not only dissolves the carnal cohesive power of sin, but utterly consumes the filthy rags of self-righteousness. The immortal spirit of man, which will stand the ordeal of death and the issues of the judgment, is unimpaired by this crucifixion; but stripped of every other hope, it clings alone to the risen Jesus, and is raised with him into a new life, and the new relation of a "fellow-citizen with the saints and of the household of God." Sometimes, to be sure, this ordeal in a measure suspends the action of the animal functions, and the subject lies apparently dead for hours. I have seen a number of cases of this sort.

The Rev. Peter Turner says it was very common among the Friendly Islanders. In a letter I recently received from him, he states, "I have seen as many as two hundred penitents lying at one time apparently dead. Their recovery was usually indicated first by the motion of their lips, and by expressions of joy and praise, such as "Precious Jesus!" "My Saviour!" "Glory to Jesus, he's pardoned my sins!" "Why did you bring me back to life? I don't want to come back to this bad world. I want to go and live with Jesus!"

Many such cases occurred in the great awakening in the north of Ireland and Scotland, principally among the Presbyterians, a few years ago.

But usually persons with some mental discipline, who have been accustomed to see and hear these things, are not the subjects of despair so deep, or emotion so strong. There is, in the experience of such, an intelligent, deliberate surrender to God, and a grateful acceptance of Jesus Christ as their Saviour on the faith of God's record concerning him; as quietly, as we may suppose, Lydia was saved.

The variety of outward manifestation, both of "godly sorrow for sin," and the joys of sins forgiven, is owing mainly to a variety of causes in the constitution, tempers, and habits of the individual subjects. They are incidental and not essential. The essential thing as I have shown, is the effective thing—"submitting," "believing," "receiving the end of our faith, even the salvation of our souls."

Allow me, my dear friend, to advertise you of the fact that, from this rugged route along which the Spirit leads the awakened sinner from Sinai to Gethsemane, Calvary, and Mount Zion, there are many by-paths that lead to the Dead Sea of utter destruction. "Gehenna, itself, where the worm dieth not and the fire is not quenched," is just at the lower extremity of Mount Zion. Unless we stick to our guide-book—the Bible—and walk steadily after our heavenly guide—the Holy Spirit —we are sure to get lost and "stumble on the dark mountains." Hence the admonition of Jesus, "Walk while ye have the light, lest darkness come upon you; for he that walketh in darkness knoweth not whither he goeth." "While ye have the light, believe in the light, that ye may be the children of light." To refuse to walk after the Spirit as did Felix and King Agrippa, or wantonly compromise with sin as did Herod Antipas, or blindly wander off in the paths of self-righteousness, so clearly defined by St. Paul, as did the Pharisees of old, and as do millions of formalists now, is not only to lose the light, and walk in darkness, but sadly to injure, and finally destroy their spiritual power of vision. The enlightenment of the world does not depend simply on an exhaustless source of light, but also on the power of vision to receive it. A man in Sydney had diseased eyes, and could not endure much light. One night, while some kind of an application was being made to his eyes, he said, "Light the candle; it has gone out." "No, the candle is burning." "It must be out, it is all darkness." Alas! his eyes were out; his power of vision was gone. "If our gospel be hid, it is hid to them that are lost"—by refusing or neglecting to walk after the Spirit—"In whom the God of this world hath blinded the minds of them which believe not, lest the light of the glorious gospel of Christ, who is the image of God, should shine unto them." I do not believe that God arbitrarily or vindictively withdraws his Spirit from anybody. It is when the sinner persists in unbelief and rebellion, till his spiritual receptivity is destroyed, and he is hopelessly "joined to his idols" that God says to his Spirit, "Let him alone." "Except ye repent ye shall all likewise perish" is the solemn warning of Jesus; but the dreadful consequences of refusing to repent, to accept the only remedy, and Saviour of sinners, represented by the word "perish," are inherent and self-entailed; relating to the moral condition of the perished sinner, rather than to God's administrative act of cutting off such a soul. The dreadful leprosy of sin in the soul is continually eating out its spiritual susceptibilities, till finally they are dead—the soul perished. The poison of the fiery serpent has diffused itself through all the life currents, and the soul is now "past feeling, having given itself over unto lasciviousness, to work all uncleanness with greediness."

Rambling through the park lands at Shane

Castle in Ireland, I stood at the root of a beautiful ash tree, and looked at it till I trembled, and said " Alas ! poor sinner, he's gone." In the early life of that tree, a little ivy crawled out from beneath its roots, and insidiously entwined itself around the body of the sapling; for years they grew together, and the stately tree seemed to luxuriate in the green foliage of the ivy. But in the course of time the ivy drew so largely on the vital resources of the tree, from earth and water, and so tightened its tenacious coil, as to obstruct the sap vessels. The noble tree declined, lingered long, but got no relief, and finally died. When I was there it was quite dead, and only remained to be plucked up by the roots. All the skill of all the gardeners, with all the fertilizers of the earth, and dews and rains of heaven, would fail to make that tree grow.

The fatal ivy of sin is in your soul, my friend; you can look within and read the sad story better than I can tell it. It must be destroyed by God's only remedy or it will destroy you.

When a soul thus perishes, what can the righteous God do with it? Such a soul could not endure the presence of God, and the purity of heaven. It cannot in justice to society be allowed to remain on earth. "God is long suffering to usward, not willing that any should perish, but that all should come to repentance;" and hence spares the sinner to the great detriment of society, as long as there is any hope in his case; but when he finally perishes. in justice aud mercy to society, the moral nuisance must be removed. This view of the subject is clearly sustained by the Saviour's standing type of hell, the Valley of Hinnom, or "Gehenna," the receptacle of all the filth of the city of Jerusalem. What was cast into the Valley of Hinnom as food for the worms and consuming fires? Nothing that could be turned to any useful account. If a horse should die in the city it would not do to leave him in the streets to diffuse effluvia and breed a pestilence. It is no use now to talk about the former beauty and value of the animal. He's dead. You can't even keep a dead man in your house, though the dearest friend you had on earth. The city authorities must in justice protect society. The dead horse is therefore dragged off by the scavengers to Hinnom. A dead soul in the commonwealth of God, unfit for heaven, no longer fit for a residence among men. The righteous ruler of the world dissolves his dishonoured connection with time, and delivers him over to the scavenger of the moral universe—the devil—who drags him down "to hell, where the worm dieth not, and the fire is not quenched." No soul is sent to hell until it has first perished by its own suicidal rebellion, and it is sent to hell because it has perished, and is hence unfit for any other place. In the literal valley, which was the type, the worms have died, and the fires have been quenched for centuries. When I was in the Valley of Hinnom it was covered with barley in the head, interspersed with olive and fig trees. It is in the real "Gehenna," the antitype, where the worms never die, and the fire is unquenchable. If the soul was annihilated, it would be nonsense to threaten it with eternal fire. So you see, my friend, the alternative of walking "after the Spirit," is to "walk after the flesh and die." "As Moses lifted up the serpent in the wilderness, even so" hath "the Son of Man" been "lifted up; that whosoever believeth on him should not perish, but have everlasting life."

Repentance in the ordinary use of the term, re-ulting in unreserved submission to God's will, is the essential preliminary to believing; but in its broad comprehensive sense, as the "godly sorrow that worketh repentance to salvation," it embraces believing.

Believing, also, in its broad saving sense as the

one grand condition of salvation, embraces, of course, the essential preliminary condition of it—repentance. As these subjects are so intimately connected with each other, I will, if you please, my friend, before we proceed to consider more at large the subject of faith, give you one simple illustration of believing, showing what a penitent sinner is to believe, and how. While I was labouring in a special series of religious services in New York, a few years ago, a policeman came into our meeting one night. He was a "detective"—they are called "spotters" there. During the preaching that night the "detective" was detected, and "reproved of sin" by God's awakening Spirit.

At the close of the prayer meeting that night he came and spoke to me, saying, "Excuse me, sir, but I would like to have a little conversation with you, if you please."

"Very good, sir, I am at your service. What is your pleasure, sir?"

"I want to know," said he, "whether the characteristics of Jesus Christ as revealed in the New Testament are Divine? I have read in the Testament of his sympathy for the suffering, his compassion for mankind, his love for his enemies, his patience with man's waywardness and persistent wickedness, his yearning desire to save sinners. I want to know whether these characteristics are divine, or whether they belong simply to his human nature?"

I was struck with the man's appearance, with his clever common sense, and especially with such a question coming from a wicked policeman—as he had confessed himself to be—right off the streets of New York; and I answered thus: "Jesus Christ was 'God manifest in the flesh,' and he manifested his Divine nature in accordance with the laws of the human intellect and heart, and hence his essential characteristics as God bore a striking resemblance to corresponding characteristics in humanity. But you will find in those characteristics—in his sympathy, his love for his enemies, his patience, his yearning desire to alleviate the woes of the world, and save sinners—an unfathomable depth that you can't find in humanity."

Through this and other short practical arguments and illustrations just to the point, we agreed in the conclusion "that those characteristics were Divine; if Divine, essential; if essential, immutable; and hence the same now as then;" "Jesus Christ the same yesterday, to-day, and for ever," as the inspired St. Paul asserts—His heart of sympathy, and love the same now, exactly as when manifest in the flesh; as really the Saviour of sinners now as then, and hence as accessible now as then; not to the natural eye, but to the intelligent faith of the penitent."

"I see it! I see it!" said he; "I never knew that before."

After a little advice as to how he should submit himself to God, believe God's testimony concerning Jesus, and on the faith of it accept Christ as his present Saviour, he bade me good night and retired.

The next night I saw him in my audience, and observed that he paid strict attention to the preaching of the gospel. At the commencement of the prayer meeting, when I invited all persons convinced of sin, who desired to enlist on their behalf, personally, the sympathy and prayers of God's people, and to converse with us, and receive personal advice to assist them in seeking their salvation, to indicate their desire by meeting us at the altar of prayer that we might have access to them, with characteristic promptness as a good policeman, he was the first man on his feet. From the rear part of the audience he walked deliberately up the aisle, and kneeled down. With hands clasped, eyes closed, and head up, his countenance manifesting, in the clear gas light of the splendidly illuminated church, the deepest agony of soul, combined with hope and firmness of purpose, he introduced, in solemn, earnest, yet subdued tones, a conversation with God. Without his knowledge I drew near and listened, and learned of him whom I had taught. His prayer made such a deep impression on my memory that I can give it almost *verbatim*.

He said, "O God, thou knowest what a wretched sinner I am! Thou knowest how I have polluted the very streets of the city with my horrible profanity! O God, thou knowest that I deserve nothing better than to be sent to hell! But, O God, I never knew till last night that the characteristics of Jesus, as revealed in the Testament, are divine. I see now that Jesus, the sinner's friend, has been loving me all the time. All through my guilty years of rebellion against thee, he has been loving me, and has been wanting all the time to save me; but I, a poor ignorant sinner, didn't know it. I just went blundering on blindly in the way to hell, and did not know that Jesus was my friend. I always hated these Methodists, and never would go among them. But, O God, I thank thee, that in thy good providence thou didst bring me here last night, and that I have learned that the characteristics of Jesus are Divine. O God, I believe it. I have read the Testament through, and I never read anywhere that Jesus ever turned any poor sinner away that came to him, and gave his case into his hands, and I don't believe he will turn me away, if I submit myself to his will. O God, thou hast helped me by thy good Spirit, I do submit my helpless, guilty soul to thee. I do believe all thou hast said about Jesus, I know he will not turn me away. Thou wilt receive me, and freely pardon my sins and save my soul for his sake. I do accept him as my Saviour."

I listened and silently prayed for his struggling soul, till I saw by his brightening countenance and the believing tone of his prayers, that he was accepting Christ as his all-sufficient present Saviour. Then I said, "O Lord, I will praise thee: though thou wast angry with me, thine anger is turned away, and thou comfortest me."

It seemed to startle him, he was having audience with God, and seemed forgetful of his surroundings, and he inquired, "What did you say, sir?" When I repeated it, he said earnestly, "Is that in the Bible?" He was ready to believe anything in the Bible, but nothing out of it pertaining to the great question at issue.

"Yes, that is in the twelfth chapter of Isaiah."

"Well, that's it. Thank God I feel that!" "O Lord," said he, "I will praise thee: though thou wast angry with me, thine anger is turned away, and thou comfortest me."

Soon after he arose and faced the audience, and testified clearly to the fact that God for Christ's sake had pardoned his sins, and filled his soul with unspeakable joy. He went home that night happy in God, called his wife and two little children together, and told them what Jesus had done for his soul, set up his family altar, and henceforth manifested in word and deed the fruits of a new life.

CHAPTER V.

EFFECTIVE CONDITION OF SALVATION—FAITH.

MY DEAR FRIEND—As faith is the one grand condition of salvation we ought to understand it. Whatever else we learn, or fail to learn; do, or fail to do—we ought to learn and do that thing on which hangs our eternal life or death. Faith, or believing—"which is faith in exercise," as the sole condition of salvation, embraces the practical end of repentance—submission to God's will—as an essential condition of its saving exercise. Jesus Christ, as before stated, hath not come to save us in our sins, nor against our will. To receive him therefore, as a Saviour, implies, in the nature of the case, a willing renunciation of sin.

That we may have an intelligible practical view of this subject, I propose to describe as briefly as practicable,—The ground, or basis of saving faith: Its object: Its natural functions: Its gracious vitality: Its end: And its demonstrative fruits.

The foundation of our faith is the gracious "purpose" of God to save mankind through the atoning merits and mediation of Jesus Christ, as revealed in the Scriptures, interprctod and applied by God the Holy Spirit. St. John, speaking of the divine works and teachings of Christ, says, "These things are written that ye might believe that Jesus is the Christ, the Son of God; and that believing ye might have life through his name." There is no instrument among men, no covenant, contract, deed, treaty of commerce or peace half so reliable, as a basis of faith, as the record of God concerning his Son, commencing with his promise to our fallen first parents, and verbally closing with his revelation to St. John on the Island of Patmos. "If we receive the witness of men, the witness of God is greater, for this is the witness of God which he hath testified of his Son."—"And this is the record, that God hath given to us eternal life, and this life is in his Son." God's first promise "that the seed of the woman should bruise the Serpent's head," to the manifestation of Messiah, extended through a period of four thousand years. Surely in that time he would reveal an adequate foundation for faith: Not very voluminous,—for then the busy multitudes of mankind could not read it, and we would have to employ lawyers to search God's records for us, and they might give us more of their own learned counsel, than of God's saving truth,—but brief, simple, and explicit. Many of its subjects are in their nature to the human mind incomprehensible, but its facts are so plain that a "wayfaring man though a fool need not err therein," yet so spiritual that the "natural man receiveth them not, neither can he know them, because they are spiritually discerned," utterly baffling the wisdom of men, but "revealed to babes," and all who with honesty of purpose seek the light of God in the paths of obedience.

We have first God's prophetic record concerning his Son. Through a period of over fifteen hundred years, "holy men of old spake as they were moved by the Holy Ghost," clearly delineating human powers and responsibility, the deep depravity of human nature, and hence the necessity of a Saviour; and all the leading facts defining his person, character, and mission. God thus advertised the world, hundreds of years in advance, when and where Messiah should be manifested;

the peculiar fact that his human nature should be born of a virgin, his unattractive person, having "no beauty that we should desire him," his humiliation, manner of life, "rejection of men," his teachings, his death, burial, resurrection, ascension, and mediation on his holy Hill of Zion. These prophetic facts were detailed with the definite distinctiveness of a history, and yet interwoven with the history of ancient cities, kingdoms, and nations, which were overthrown hundreds of years before Christ, according to the predictions of those very prophets, so that their remote antiquity is proved beyond successful contradiction.

We have, second, the historical record of God concerning his Son.

These foretold facts as they transpired in the person and ministry of Christ were recorded at the time of their occurrence, and during the lifetime of the masses of men and women who witnessed them. The men inspired by the Holy Ghost to record these facts, and the conditions on which "men's sins should be forgiven or retained," were divinely accredited by miraculous "signs and wonders." The men, their mission, their gospel facts, and those attesting signs from God, were all subjects of immediate record, which was published far and wide among their enemies. The great central miracle and saving fact—the resurrection of Christ, for example—was at once proclaimed by the living witnesses of it, when their testimony would have been challenged, and their statements, if not true, refuted. Their testimony implicated the Jewish people in the murder of their long-looked for Messiah. Peter thus charged it home upon them right there, where but a few weeks before they had executed Him. "The God of Abraham, and of Isaac, and of Jacob, the God of our fathers, hath glorified his Son Jesus, whom ye delivered up, and denied him in the presence of Pilate, when he was determined to let him go. But ye denied the Holy One and the Just, and desired a murderer to be granted unto you; and killed the Prince of Life, whom God hath raised from the dead; whereof we are witnesses." And there, before their eyes, was attesting proof of these facts in the miraculous healing of the lame man who was "leaping and praising God in Solomon's porch." If these things had not been so the Jewish people would have refuted them at once, and being so numerous and widely scattered throughout the Roman world their refutation would have been circulated more rapidly and widely than the Gospels could have been. The

Jewish people are present in all parts of the world now, and just as eager as ever to find a refutation of these facts; and yet they have never been able to produce a better one than the attempted refuting testimony of the bribed soldiers—"His disciples came and stole him away while we slept." What court would receive the testimony of witnesses to what they affirmed as having occurred while they were asleep? Nay, so far from being able to refute these gospel facts, tens of thousands of Jews during the lifetime of these witnesses believed and were saved.

These facts with their divine attestations were submitted to the all-conquering Romans and learned Greeks who would have refuted them, and published the refutation throughout the world if they had not been true. After St. Paul, in all the principal cities in Syria, Asia Minor, Macedonia, and Achaia, had been proclaiming a crucified and risen Christ for at least twenty-five years, in writing from the city of Ephesus to the church in Corinth, records this great fact:—"For I delivered unto you first of all that which I also received, how that Christ died for our sins according to the Scriptures: And that he was buried, and that he rose again the third day according to the Scriptures: And that he was seen of Cephas, then of the twelve; After that he was seen of above five hundred brethren at once; of whom the greater part remain unto this present, but some are fallen asleep. After that he was seen of James; then of all the apostles. And last of all he was seen of me also, as of one born out of due time." Here were "about five hundred men," all concurring in their testimony to the same great facts, which they had seen with their eyes, and proclaimed in the very teeth of their enemies, through a period of over a quarter of a century, almost to the utmost limits of the Roman world.

Not one of them could have had the least motive for asserting these things if they had not been true, for their testimony exposed them to the loss of everything in this world, even life itself, for the mass of them finally sealed their testimony with their own blood. In view of the bloody persecutions they endured for Christ, they could truly say with their fellow martyr, St. Paul, "If in this life only we have hope in Christ, we are of all men most miserable."

There was ample time, we see, for challenging these witnesses, and refuting their testimony if it had been possible.

They constituted no small faction, unworthy of the attention of the great and learned of those days, for their movement shook the foundation of empires, and "The kings of the earth set themselves, and the rulers took counsel together against the Lord, and against his anointed." Yet such was the incontestable character of these facts, though directly opposed to the carnal nature of men, and the popular institutions of those days, the learned Greeks and the masses of the Roman world gradually succumbed to the power of gospel truth, and notwithstanding the degenerating tendencies of human nature, the Asiatic and European countries that received the gospel from these personal witnesses of the resurrection of Christ, are in the main, at least, nominally Christian countries to this day.

Moreover, we have the testimony of Jewish and heathen historians, the avowed enemies of the Gospel, corroborating its leading facts. Josephus, who was an active leader in those wars which resulted in the destruction of Jerusalem about A.D. 70, speaks of John the Baptist as a good man and a preacher of righteousness, and of Herod's sin in putting him to death. He also mentions Pilate as having been the Roman Governor of Judea about that time.

The younger Pliny, who was a Roman Governor in Bithynia about the year A.D. 107, writes to the Emperor Trajan inquiring how he should deal with the Christians, who, in great numbers, were accused at his tribunal of their "superstition." He admits that the only charge against them was that they were worshippers of Christ, and assembled together to sing hymns to him. The Emperor replied that he "had better not seek them out, but that if brought before him, they must be capitally punished unless they will renounce their superstition." This was but a continuance of the persecutions that raged during the ministrations of the Apostles.

Tacitus, the historian, who wrote about the year 110, says, "Nero brought forward, as accused persons, to be subjected to the most exquisite punishments, those who were commonly called Christians. The author of this sect, Christ, was capitally punished by the procurator, Pontius Pilate, while Tiberius was Emperor."

Suetonius, a contemporary Roman historian with Tacitus, says :—"The Christians, followers of a new superstition, were punished." He also, in writing of the reign of Claudius, says, that "that Emperor expelled all the Jews from Rome, because they raised continual tumults at the instigation of Christ." He no doubt heard Christ spoken of as we do now in the present tense, and supposed him to be then the ringleader of the sect bearing his name. This is doubtless the banishment of Jews from Rome that St. Paul mentions, which drove "Aquila and Priscilla from Rome" to Corinth.

Lucian also, another Heathen writer of the second century, says of the Christians, "They still worship that great man who was crucified in Palestine, because he introduced into the world this new religion."

The Emperor Julian speaks of "Jesus, the Nazarene:" "Jesus whom you celebrate was one of Cæsar's subjects;" and tauntingly addressing Christians says :—"You are so very unhappy as to leave the immortal gods, and go over to the dead man of the Jews." Speaking of the time, he says, "These things happened in the days of Tiberius and Claudius." In Nero's day, says Tacitus, "a vast multitude were apprehended, and their sufferings were aggravated by insult and mockery; some were disguised in skins of wild beasts and worried to death by dogs. others crucified; others wrapped in pitchy sheets, and set on fire in the night to serve as an illumination." Nero illuminated his gardens with them. It should be observed that, though these authors penned these facts in the beginning of the second century, the authors themselves, in the main, lived through the latter half of the first century, contemporaneously with many of those personal witnesses of Christ's resurrection.

Without going into the details of the argument to support the inspiration and divine authority of the Holy Scriptures from the various classes of evidence, external, internal, collateral, and demonstrative, which our space will not allow, suffice it to say that they are so clear and conclusive as to challenge any honest man, Jew, Mohammedan, Boodhist, infidel, or sceptic, to an investigation and personal test of their divine origin and saving power.

Dr. Freshman, a learned Jewish rabbi in Canada, was attending the meeting of an assembly of learned Jews in the city of Montreal. The president of that assembly, or council, was a learned rabbi from Jerusalem.

During the progress of their deliberations, Dr. Freshman asked the Chairman this question : "If our ancient prophets did foretell all the great leading, events that should occur in the world's history—and we believe they did—how did it come to pass that they entirely overlooked and gave us no notice of that most remarkable of all events—the advent of Jesus of Nazareth and the Christian Dispensation?"

The learned doctor in the chair, after some hesitation and evident embarrassment, replied, "When I return to Jerusalem, I will examine the records and let you know."

Whether he instituted an examination of the Jewish records in Jerusalem, or not, was never known to Dr. Freshman. He received no answer to his question, and it led him to search the sacred records for himself. The result was "he believed" and was saved, and has been for a number of years a successful Wesleyan minister of the Canada Conference. He has, for the last three or four years, been establishing a German Wesleyan church in the city of Hamilton. I have the pleasure of a personal acquaintance with the doctor and his family, and can testify to his intelligent zeal and usefulness as a brother beloved in Christ.

So any man, willing to know and obey the truth will certainly find it by searching the

Scriptures and yielding obedience to their instructions.

I became acquainted with a very intelligent Jew in the city of Montreal. His father, I was informed, was a wealthy banker in Germany. I heard this Jew relate his Christian experience in a fellowship meeting, the substance of which was, in his broken English, this—"The Spirit of de Lord take hold of my heart in my fader's house, in Germany. He make me feel so bad I could not eat my food or take my rest.

"My fader say to me, 'Why you no be happy? You mope round, just so miserable as can be. Plenty of money, why you no be happy?'

"I say 'Fader, I find no place for my soul. De money wont buy a place for my soul. I lie down and die one day, and den what good de money to me, and where go my poor soul?'

"By-and-by I reads in a paper about one, Dr. Freshman, a Jewish rabbi in Canada dat find Messiah. I says to myself, 'I go to Canada to find dat rabbi dat find Messiah.' When I come to Canada, I ask de first thing, 'Where is Dr. Freshman?' and dey tell me dat he live in de city Hamilton. When I go to de city of Hamilton he not at home. I no find him for two weeks.

Then one man show him to me at a public meeting, and I look at him till de meeting was out, and as he come, I say to him, 'You Dr. Freshman?'

"'Yes.'

"'You Jewish rabbi?'

"'Yes.'

"'You find Messiah?'

"'Yes.'

"'Well, you give me two lessons, and I pay you.'

"Dr. Freshman say, 'Come to my house, and I give you many lessons, and not charge anyting.'

"But I say, 'O no, Dr. Freshman, I no want you to teach me for notting.'

"Den I go to Dr. Freshman, and he talk to me, and talk to me, and talk to me; but I no find Messiah,

"Den I go to de Catolic church, and talk to de priest to find Messiah.

"De priest, he tell me about de baptism and de holy water; and I say, 'Go away wid your water. I wants to find a place for my soul.'

"Den I go back to Dr. Freshman, and he say, 'You Hebrew scholar. Now, take your Hebrew Bible and read what our ancient prophets say about

Messiah. Take your pen and write down de exact description dey give of him, especially the fifty-third chapter of Isaiah; and when you get de prophetic directions how to find Messiah, take your Greek Testament and search, and you will find, as face answers face in a glass, so de New Testament answers to de Old, and dat everything de old prophets say about Messiah was fulfilled exactly in de person of Jesus of Nazaret. When your judgment be convinced, den bow down on your knees and pray to Got in the name of Jesus, and you find Messiah in your heart. He save you from all your sins.'

"So I follow de instructions dat Dr. Freshman he did give me, and my judgment he get convinced, and I bow down on my knees and I cry, 'O Got of Abraham, Isaac, and Jacob, Got of my faders, I pray to dee in the name of dy dear suffering Son Jesus Christ. I be convinced from dy holy books of the Old and New Testaments dat He be Messiah which dow has sent into de world to save sinners. Dow knows what a great sinner I am; but Jesus 'comes to save de chief of sinners.' I trust my soul to him. I believe he can save me. O Got have mercy on my poor soul, and save me from my sins, for Jesus' sake. I believe all dow has say about Jesus, and I take him as my Saviour.'

"While I pray I feel more and more bad, and I tot my poor soul he must go to hell! Den, I say, if Jesus Christ bore my sins in his own body, and redeemed my soul with his own blood, my soul he no need to go to hell. Den I give my soul to Jesus. I believe in Jesus, and just so quick as lightning I finds Messiah! He save me from my sins, he fill my soul wid unspeakable joy! My soul he find a home in Jesus! He abide in Jesus now for tree years, and I know him more and more, and love him wid all my heart." He proceeded to tell of some remarkable answers to prayer he had experienced, and such was the artless simplicity of his story, and the light and unction of the Holy Spirit shining through his broken utterances, that between laughing and weeping for joy, when he sat down there were but few dry eyes in that large assembly. He was at that time employed as a colporteur and Bible-reader to his people of different languages in the city of Montreal.

The oracles of God, my friend, as a basis for saving faith, are entirely adequate for Jew and Gentile. Some learned men, to be sure, have written against the Scriptures, but their powers were employed, not to find out the truth, but to find difficulties and objections to it. When men go into an exploration of God's works or teachings for the purpose of finding difficulties and objections, they can always be accommodated.

Some infidel writers were really battling against corrupt forms of Christianity, a fruitful source of infidelity, and knew but little about the Bible, and nothing of the Holy Spirit's power attending it.

Those of them who should have known better, were among the "wise and prudent," who practically ignore the personal presence of the Holy Spirit, and His teaching and saving offices, and so "lean to their own understanding" that "these things are hid from their eyes." Their blindness is such, that they either refute their own arguments, or fall into egregious blunders that expose their ignorance of spiritual things, and in bitterest remorse and despair they pass away, "but the word of the Lord endureth for ever."

Bishop Colenso's fallacious dodge is to locate his premises so remotely in geography, chronology, and history, that the masses of the people have no immediate opportunity of ascertaining the character of the pretended facts embraced in his assumptions. The learned prelate states them in such a bold confident way that many forget to inquire whether or not "the things are so." Admitting his premises, they cannot escape his logical conclusions. But as attention is called to the grounds of his arguments, the world finds out that the bishop is guilty of what logicians call "begging the question"—assuming as the basis of his arguments, not admitted facts, or well defined defensible grounds of truth, but bold, unproved, unadmitted statements of his own.

For example, we read in the 27th and 28th chapters of Deuteronomy the command of Moses for the assembling of the tribes of Israel in the valley between Mount Ebal and Mount Gerizim, and that the blessings of the law should be proclaimed by six heralds, representing six tribes, from Mount Gerizim, and the curses of the law in like manner from Mount Ebal, and on each announcement the people should say "Amen." We read in the 8th chapter of Joshua that the whole thing occurred, "as Moses the servant of the Lord had commanded before, according to all that was written in the book of the law."

But Bishop Colenso, from his stand-point in Africa, insinuates, in accordance with his wily mode of assuming the premises of his arguments, that it never occurred; that, the thing is in itself a physical impossibility, for the people of Israel could not find standing room between those mountains; and even if they could, the heralds could not be heard from the two opposite mountains, and therefore the Bible narrative is not true.

Now what are the facts? In exploring those "old paths" I sent a young Arab to ascend Mount Ebal, about fifty feet above the level of the valley, while I, meantime, ascended the more precipitous steeps of Mount Gerizim, to about the same elevation. We stood then at a distance from each other, as I ascertained approximately by stepping it, of about four hundred yards.

I proclaimed several passages of Scripture, one of which was, "Ho, every one that thirsteth, come ye to the waters, and he that hath no money; come ye, buy and eat; yea, come, buy wine and milk without money and without price." I then sang the "Beautiful World," a song he had never heard in the world before, yet he was able to tell me every passage I quoted, and repeat the chorus of the hymn I sang.

That afternoon was not a favourable time for such an experiment because of a strong breeze from the north-west drawing directly across the line of sound between us, but notwithstanding that, he heard my utterances, and I heard his responses.

Moreover, there were embarrassments with us that did not exist in the great event itself. The said young man, a native of Shechem, was not familiar with my voice nor with my language. Though he had been for some time in Bishop Gobat's high school on Mount Zion, his knowledge of the English colloquial was very imperfect. He could not anticipate any of my utterances, for I had not even hinted to him in advance what I would say.

The Jewish people, on the other hand, were perfectly acquainted with the voices of their heralds, their language, and the subject matter of their announcements. The mass of the people had no doubt known from memory the blessings and curses of the law of Moses from the time they were little boys and girls, and there by the altar of God on Mount Ebal, "on great stones set up," were written "all the words of this law very plainly." They assembled to hear these proclaimed in their order, and even if those on the outskirts could not have heard distinctly, they knew what was proclaimed, and could join in the universal response "Amen!" So we find that the physical impossibility raised by Dr. Colenso as a fulcrum for his sceptical lever by which to overthrow the temple of God's imperishable truth, is not an impossibility at all, but entirely practicable.

The fact is, sound in that country travels with a facility that a man in Africa would not be likely to appreciate.

As it regards the other horn of this difficulty, the incapacity of the valley, I may simply remark that if we could be heard four hundred yards across the valley, we could be heard the same distance right and left. That will give us an area four by eight hundred yards, with any amount of elbow room, the valley being over a league in length. But the space above defined will give us two millions eight hundred and eighty thousand square feet.

Learned men agree that the whole nation of the Israelites at that time did not exceed two millions. A command for a general assembly of the tribes for the purposes of worship, or war, necessarily exempted the sick, and all who were required to take care of the sick and to "stay with the stuff," —their immense herds and household effects. In a country like that, so subject to Bedouin marauders, with two and a half of the tribes living east of Jordan, probably one half of the population would necessarily be exempt on this religious occasion. Such a necessary exemption was so palpable, that in the greatest emergencies of war there was a law, that they who stayed with the stuff should share equally in the spoils of war with those who "went up to the battle." The people on this great occasion were all represented by their "elders, officers, and judges, who stood on this side of the ark and on that side, before the priests and Levites, which bare the ark of the covenant of the Lord," and "all Israel" not exempt by necessities provided for by law, altogether numbering possibly a million, or at most a million and a half, for whom standing closely we have within our defined lines nearly three millions square feet. Many of the small women and children would not occupy over a square foot each. So this impossibility, like its fellow, turns out to be entirely practicable, and if the number of the Israelites was so small as Dr. Colenso would make it appear in another line of his fallacious argumentation, we could slip them in half the space.

But, my dear friend, I would specially remind you of the fact, that it is not essential to the salvation of a sinner that he acquire a knowledge of all the variety and extent of God's testimony concerning his Son, nor the various classes of evidence employed to support and defend it against the assaults of infidelity; nor the mysteries involved in the subjects embraced in it; nor the difficult, knotty questions the learned metaphysicians and sceptics may raise. The sinner, under the enlightening quickening power of the Holy Spirit, should seek the Lord, "if haply they might feel after him, and find him;" for "he is not far from every one of us," through the teaching medium of palpable facts.

First, the fact of his own being. How came he into existence, and for what purpose?

Second, the existence of the universe, as manifested to his senses; and hence its Creator, "For the invisible things of him from the creation of the world are clearly seen, being understood by the things that are made, even his eternal power and godhead, so that they are without excuse."

Third, a recognition of God's great law of demand and supply, so unvarying in its manifestation, that to find a real demand is to be assured of an ample and available supply. He consciously possesses a threefold nature:—

1st. A corporeal body with its demands, and a supply for these demands—food, water, air, light, and all the rest.

2nd. An intellectual nature, and the most ample and compensative field for its exercise.

3rd. A spiritual nature adapted to moral relationships and to moral law pertaining to this life, and to his Creator, and the invisible world; hence his aspirations to rise above the mists of time to an unclouded vision of eternity; to hold intercourse with the invisible and spiritual.

This demand is so potent, and so prominent in the experience of mankind, that any new mysterious thing that holds out any hope of a supply, is sure to attract a mass of anxious inquiries, and hence the success of all the mystery-mongers, from the witch of Endor down to Mr. Davis the "spirit rapper."

In the department of man's spiritual nature there is his "religiousness" disposing him to be a worshipper, while he may clearly see that there is nothing in this world worthy of his worship. It is readily excited by the power of poetry and song.

A leading function of his spiritual nature is his conscience—a teacher, a lawgiver, a witness, a recorder, a judge, an executioner; hence the universal struggle of mankind to square accounts with conscience: Hence the ancient heathen temples, and hecatombs of slain beasts, and all the varieties of modern expedients among Heathen, Mohammedans, Jews, and formal Christians. Though some men may in word deny the existence of their spiritual nature, and its conscious demands, yet they can't ignore nor conceal the fact, and any man may intelligently learn that the supply for these spiritual demands of his being does not exist in visible or material things: hence the clear presumption, that the God who made him, and endowed him with these various powers, and provided so amply for the inferior demands of his being, pertaining to this life, would reveal an available supply, for the superior demands of his being, pertaining to "things unseen and eternal."

We have just such a revelation in the Bible, another palpable fact. Let the infidel account for its existence. Whatever mysteries and difficulties it may furnish for the speculative critic, the seeking sinner has simply to do with its facts. Its delineatory facts of human responsibility, guilt, corruption, condemnation, and bondage, have their counterpart and demonstration in his own experience. Its saving facts have a demonstration in the experience and lives of Christians, who have proved them by experience, and bear a clear testimony to them.

He also consciously feels the awakening influence of the Spirit, whose personal presence, and interest in him, he may not at all appreciate, but he knows that the influence he feels is foreign to himself, and tends to lead him from sin to God, and must hence proceed from God, and is proof of God's desire to save him. All these facts combine to induce him to come directly to the God who made him, in the name of his Son Jesus Christ, and personally test the truth of his gospel, and demonstrate its saving power in his own experience. He may not know a letter of the alphabet, but feels these facts, and hears these gospel truths proclaimed from the pulpit, or from the lips of a child, yields obedience, and experiences salvation through faith in Jesus. The testimony of living witnesses has a great deal to do in this work of leading souls to Christ.

A worldly unbelieving man in the state of Indiana who was awakened by the Spirit, sought and found peace with God, Soon after another infidel neighbour, who had confidence in his veracity, waited on him, and said, "You know, sir, that I am an unbeliever of the Bible as a revelation from God, and have always looked upon churches as organized forms of superstition, but I learn that you profess to have found access to God, and have received a pardon from Him for all your sins. This is all strange to me; but I believe you to be a man of truth, and if you candidly tell me that such are the facts in your experience, I cannot doubt your testimony. And if you will tell me how I too may gain access to God, and have my sins forgiven, I will take your advice and do anything to attain such a result."

The other assured him, on the honour of a man and a Christian, that such were the facts in his experience, and succeeded within a few days in leading his infidel friend to Jesus, and heard him testify to the saving facts of the Gospel as he had also experienced them.

A young lawyer in New Jersey, an avowed infidel, went to a fellowship meeting of Christians "to write down their experiences to furnish sport for his friends in the office." You will rarely find a good lawyer an infidel, and never when they bring their trained powers of analysis to an honest investigation of the evidences of Christianity. The said young lawyer, being personally acquainted with the names and general character of most of the Christians present, entered their names in his note-book, and wrote out their facts as they delivered them, till he had recorded, in the most business-like way, the testimony of eighteen witnesses, when he suddenly waked up to the subject, and said to himself, "These are credible witnesses —men and women who would not lie. I would not want any better witnesses in court to substantiate any matter of fact within their knowledge. They have not testified to what they think, or hope, or believe simply, but to facts in their experience, which they say they know. To ignore such testimony is to ignore the laws of evidence—a thing I dare not attempt." With that he arose, and confessed all these facts in his case, and begged the good people to pray for him, that he might be enabled to believe and be saved. He was soon after converted to God, and became himself a witness for Jesus.

When I was labouring in Ballaarat two years ago, where a multitude of souls were saved, a sceptic about fifty years old, or upwards, was brought to a saving knowledge of the truth. In his own peculiar, blunt, but clever mode of expressing himself, he subsequently said, in a fellowship meeting, and in a letter to me personally, "Friends, I want to preface my experience with a confession. I would like to confess to all these Methodists, and to all the Methodists in the world, if I could, how I have hated and abused them. I didn't believe in Christianity at all, but I especially hated the Methodists. I thought they were the greatest humbugs in the world, and tried as far as I could to make everybody else think so. I came to these meetings through the persuasion of a friend. I can't say that I had any curiosity to hear the stranger. I had heard a great many preachers, and cared nothing for any of them; but to gratify my friend I came. My attention was at once arrested, my prejudices allayed, and when I heard the Gospel presented as a practical common sense thing, and that any sinner may test its truth, and demonstrate its saving power in his own heart, I said to myself, 'That's a proposition that commends itself to my conscience—a subject involving my eternity of being for happiness or misery brought within the demonstrable range of my own experience, and testing power! I can't ignore such a proposition without doing violence to my own common sense and conscience. I have a turn for demonstration, and I'll prove this thing, I have had many a discussion with ministers and others, and they have given me some terrible twistings, but they never shook a pin of my infidelity; but now I'll test this thing, and prove that it is either true or false. From these considerations my mind was set at once to try it, and without any special emotional feeling, I went and bowed down at that altar. When I kneeled there and looked the Lord Almighty in the face for about an hour, ah then I saw and felt that God's revealed facts about my dreadful heart-wickedness, my bondage to sin and Satan, my exposure to penalty, were true. If true so far, why not true all the way through? So I just followed the instructions of my teacher with the simplicity of a child, and worked it out—a clear demonstration of consciousness in less than twenty-four hours. Before, I was worse than a heathen; now I 'know that I have passed from death unto life.' I know that I have peace with God through our Lord Jesus Christ, and I'm happy in God every day." I received a letter from him the next morning after he had gone forward to the altar of prayer; but before I had time to reply, or see him, he surrendered his soul to God, believed God's "record concerning His Son," and on the faith of it accepted Jesus, and was saved. Nine months afterwards, returning to Ballaarat I found this man steadfast in faith, "and increasing in the knowledge and love of God." I learned from some of his neighbours that he had up to that time been instrumental in leading seven persons to Christ. I saw him again but a few months ago, and heard last week that he is making good progress in spiritual life. Another much older man, I remember at the same meeting, "believed on the Lord Jesus Christ," and amid his shouts of praise to God for saving him, I heard him exclaim, "I have been a faithful servant of the Devil for sixty-eight years." That man has passed through extraordinary trials and sufferings since, but is firmly anchored in Christ. I merely mention these as specimen illustrations of the demonstrative character of Gospel truth and saving power in Jesus.

The Australasian Conference at its last session (1865) reported an increase for that Conference year, in members and probationers, numbering five thousand six hundred and thirty-six persons, nearly all of whom had borne a testimony to the pardoning mercy of God in their own experience.

I encountered an infidel on a New Zealand

steamship, some time since, and having gone through the different classes of evidence, proving the divine authority of the Bible, I gave him many examples of persons whose testimony could not be disputed, and told him also my own experience on the subject. "Well," said he, "I am only thirty-two years old, and I don't know but I will come round to your side yet."

With that Colonel R., who had heard but a little of the discussion on the last point, said, "I am a Christian, but I can't admit the argument from experience, for Mahomedans and Boodhists profess the same thing."

"Nay, Colonel R.," I replied, "that is begging the question. I don't grant your premises. Jesus says to all poor sinners, 'Come unto me, all ye that labour and are heavy laden, and I will give you rest. Take my yoke upon you, and learn of me, for I am meek and lowly of heart'—kind, sympathising, approachable, 'and ye shall find rest for your souls.' Penitent sinners accept this call, come to Jesus by faith, find rest for their souls; and in life and in death bear a distinct testimony to the fact. Now, that is just what the heathen and Mahomedans, and all classes of merely formal Christians, do not find; and hence the multiplication of their shrines, penances, and pilgrimages, just as the old Athenian heathens multiplied their gods. They go to one altar and find no rest, then to another, and another, seeking rest and finding none, except the satisfaction that a dying man has in the reflection that he spared no pains to try to save himself from death. Millions of souls, keenly conscious of their burden of sin and misery, spend weary years in 'going about to establish their own righteousness,' till they drop into the grave, or in utter desperation try to expiate their guilt and find rest for their souls by swinging on hooks fastened into their flesh, and all manner of torture down to the crushing of the wheels of Juggernaut; and though many became stoics in patient suffering, yet in all this vale of woe and death, not one scintillation of light is seen, or one word of testimony heard, to assure us that they found 'rest for their souls.'" As I was going on with my facts, the Colonel said, "Excuse me, Sir, I must go on deck," and suddenly departed.

Nay, my friend, the testimony of living Christians to facts is not to be invalidated by the negative testimony of mere formalists and heathens. There are millions of men who can testify that though they have travelled a great deal, they never saw California; but that weighs nothing against my statement of fact that I have spent years there. Or, if they say, "O yes, we found California in Africa," any schoolboy can see that they were mistaken.

The blind leaders of these blind millions who are trying to work their passage to heaven, well know that their prescriptions will not give rest to their souls, and hence are always prepared to meet their disappointment by reminding them of some one of a thousand things they have failed to do, and excite their hopes in a future saving work to be performed, and keep them going. In the Holy Land, for example, there is a shrine for nearly every prophet that ever lived. Even the tomb of Moses is visited and worshipped in the mountains west of Jordan, between the Dead Sea, and "Santa Saba." At that great Greek fortress—the "Convent of Santa Saba"—in the mountains between the Dead Sea and Bethlehem, a hundred skulls of monks, said to have been murdered by the Persians many years ago, are shown through the grating of a sacred crypt, but three of them are left within reach of pious pilgrims, who have kissed those skulls till they glisten with the wear of the lips of successive generations of weary and heavy laden souls, seeking rest and finding it not, because they came not to Jesus. This is but an illustration of the various modes of millions of Jews and Gentiles at the present day, who are trying in vain to meet the conscious demands of their spiritual nature apart from God's only provision. But the experience of true believers, as summed up by St. Peter, is a different thing altogether. "Whom having not seen, ye love (says he); in whom, though now ye see him not, yet believing, ye rejoice with joy unspeakable, and full of glory, receiving the end of your faith"—the very thing they sought by faith—"even the salvation of your souls;" and all that, too according to God's prophetic advertisement of "the sufferings of Christ, and the glory that should follow."

So you see, my friend, the demonstrative argument of the truth of the Bible, and the saving power of Jesus, based on the experience, and embodied in the testimony of millions of credible witnesses, is unanswerable. "We know," says St. John, of all true believers, "that we have passed from death unto life." What we know, all mankind may know. Our experience demonstrates what is the privilege of every sinner. Hence, every unbeliever who ever heard the Gospel will be left utterly without excuse; and when he stands at the bar of God, he will not say to his judge, "I read some infidel books, and could not answer their objections, and I could not solve the mysteries of the gospel record." Such excuses would not touch the point at all. He did know that he was a poor sinner. He did know that the gospel proclaimed an Almighty Saviour of sinners. He did know that he was invited times without number to come to him and "find rest for his soul." And worse than all, he knew that he wilfully and persistently refused to "come to him that he might have life." He will stand "speechless" before God, and the King shall say to his executioners, "Bind him hand and foot, and take him away, and cast him into outer darkness; there shall be weeping and gnashing of teeth."

CHAPTER VI.

OBJECT: NATURAL FUNCTIONS, AND SPIRITUAL GIFT OF FAITH.

THE object of faith, my dear friend, is not any particular creed, or theological system, or peculiar form of biblical criticism, but the living Saviour himself. Whatever a man's particular creed may be, however mixed up with damaging speculative dogmas or traditional practical errors, however much or little he may know about the grounds of evidence, in the Holy Scriptures, in regard to Christ, or to the testimony of living witnesses, if he is led by the awakening Spirit of God to realize his guilt, condemnation under the law, pollution, bondage, and helplessness, and will confess his sins, consent to renounce them, surrender his helpless soul to God, and on the faith of what he may have read or heard of Jesus, accept him as his Saviour, that moment he will receive salvation in Christ. It is not a matter of indifference whether he know much or little on the subject. It is a great advantage to gain all the knowledge possible on the subject; but simple saving faith requires essentially no more than the knowledge of the experimental facts of the sinner's wretchedness and need, and such knowledge of the only Saviour of sinners as will lead him to abandon all hope in everything else, and cling to Jesus as did sinking Peter, or as a drowning man to the last spar.

As before shown, there cannot be the exercise of saving faith without "repentance towards God." "He shall be called Jesus, for he shall save his people from their sins;" not in their sins, nor against their will. To receive Christ, therefore, as a Saviour from sin, implies, in the nature of the case, a hearty consent to a divorce from all sin. The point of unreserved submission to God's will—to give up everything opposed to his will, and accept his will as the rule of heart and life—is the end to be attained by repentance. It is a matter of no moment how long, or how short, the penitential struggle, if it bring the sinner to that essential point. It is an utter impossibility—a self contradiction—for him savingly to accept

Christ till he does reach this position of unreserved submission to the will of God, but the sooner he reach it the better; and having reached it, whether by ten years' or ten minutes' repentance, let him just there and then "believe in the Lord Jesus Christ," and he will certainly be saved.

The natural functions of faith embrace all those powers of mind, heart, and will, essential to natural faith in all mutual human relationships. It comprises—*first*, the exercise of perception, conception, reason, and judgment; *second*, the conscience with its various exercises; *thirdly*, the will with its various forms of manifestation, combining the complex exercise of the intellectual and moral nature, assenting, consenting, appropriating, in accordance with the natural laws of credence and acceptance. "Faith cometh by hearing, and hearing by the Word of God." The demand calling it into exercise is the consciousness of need; the supply is revealed in the Gospel. The sinner reads or hears that God hath provided a ransom, a remedy—an almighty, available Saviour. He assents to the facts, consents to the terms, accepts Christ in accordance with the most simple common sense laws of natural faith. Any measure of faith short of the appropriating act embracing Christ as a present Saviour, falls short of saving faith. Say, for illustration, that a town is visited by some dreadful disease. The lists of mortality are swelling daily with fearful rapidity, and no remedy seems in the least to check its death-dealing progress, when suddenly a celebrated physician arrives, who is said to be perfectly acquainted with the horrible disease and its treatment, and never lost a case. The attention of the public is arrested, and the first inquiry is to know if a man with such professions of skill has indeed arrived; and secondly, on what he founds his pretensions. He promptly submits his papers for inspection. It turns out that he has a diploma from the best medical college in Europe, and the written and verbal testimony of many living witnesses who have been cured through his skill—an adequate basis for faith in the said doctor.

Some read his papers all over, consider them well, and say but little, but can't question their genuineness. Others read but a portion of them, and assent to them as everything that could be desired. Others cannot read, or have no time for a personal examination, but from the testimony of those who have investigated the matter, and especially of those who have been cured by him, they are fully convinced of the unquestionable skill of the physician. All that is merely the faith of the head—an essential thing so far as it goes, but of itself saves nobody. That is the character of the faith of millions of nominal Christians. They have thoroughly examined "the record of God concerning his Son," and assent to the whole of it, yet remain in their sins.

Now let us see the practical operation of the various degrees and qualities of faith in these sick men.

One poor fellow says:—"I'm very sick. I can't tell how it may go with me. I must get relief or die. I have heard a great deal about that wonderful doctor, and I daresay it is all truth; but there's our old family physician under whose treatment my father died; I don't like to cast him off. I had rather trust my case in his hands than risk a stranger."

Another says:—"Dear me, if I don't get relief soon, I know not what will become of me. I have a great mind to send for that celebrated physician, but I have some medicine in the house that is said to be very good, and it's all paid for; I will try it and see if I can get relief without sending for that doctor."

Another says:—"I'm in a bad way. Go and see

that great doctor, and tell him how I am, and ask him if he will undertake to cure me, and allow me to continue the daily use of pickles, preserves, tobacco, and rum, and take such portions of his medicine as I like. I have great faith in that doctor; and if he will undertake to cure me on those conditions, I'll employ him at once."

One says, "I'm very ill! Send for that doctor." The doctor is promptly at his side. "Doctor," says the dying man, "what about those credentials of yours? I am very sick, and I am afraid you cannot cure me." The doctor kindly gives him the best grounds of evidence, and tries to stimulate his hope and faith. The man replies, "that all looks very well, and I cannot question the truth of what you say, but somehow I cannot believe in you; we hear of so many deceivers in the world, and"——exit doctor, and away on his mission of mercy among those who believe in him.

Another says: "Oh! I feel so cold, and bad, and lifeless. Oh! I must try and get some relief; and then I'll send for that doctor."

There is another who is piteously crying—"O Doctor, do come and save me! Do save me!" but will not give his case into the hands of the physician, or submit to treatment.

But here's a common-sense man, who cries out

"I'm a dying man! Send for that doctor as soon as you can. Tell him to come to me as quickly as possible!" "O Doctor, I'm in a dreadful state. If I don't get relief I must certainly die. I have tried all sorts of available remedies, and am getting worse and worse. I have no faith in any of them, but I have faith in you, Doctor. I satisfied my mind as to your skill before I sent for you. I give my case unreservedly into your hands. I consent to your treatment. Do with me just as you like, but save me if you can. I have faith, Doctor, to believe that you can save me; and I know you will do your best. Save me, if you can. I trust my life in your hands."

Now I need scarcely add that all those cases, except the last, which represent so many different classes of sinners, would die a miserable death. The said doctor did not destroy any of them, but in their neglect, or refusal to employ him, they are destroyed by the common plague, fatal to so many thousands in the town; but all who fully commit themselves to the care, and cheerfully submit to the treatment of the great physician, are saved.

Sometimes painful operations are necessary, requiring a little time, great decision, and patience; but steadfast practical faith will triumph, not by any intrinsic power of its own, but by its simple confidence in the physician's skill, and hearty acquiescence in the doctor's own application of it.

I heard the Rev. Granville Moody, late Colonel of the Ohio 74th, say: "When a youth in Baltimore city, my mother, laying her hand on my shoulder, said, 'My son, what lump is this on your shoulder-blade?' 'I do not know mother; I have felt something there for some time.'" Dr. Smith, a celebrated surgeon, was sent for, and pronounced it a very dangerous "*exostosis*." Some remedies were applied, but it steadily increased in size. The doctor then said it would require the "scalpel and the saw."

Young Moody hesitated, but a lady sent for him, and examining it, said, "Oh! it is that dreadful thing that killed my dear husband. I begged him to submit to an operation, but could not get his courage up to bear the pain, and it grew on, and killed him. O Mr. Moody, you are a young man, and ought to submit to any thing that would save your precious life. O do, I beseech you, for your own sake, and for the sake of your dear parents, do let Dr. Smith operate on it. It will be but a few hours of dreadful agony, and, then, perhaps, a long life of usefulness."

"Her tears and eloquence of persuasion nerved me up," said Granville, and I said to her, "'I'll do it!'"

"On the day appointed," continued Moody, "the doctor came, in company with a number of young medical students. His surgical instruments were spread out on my mother's large tea-board. My parents and all the family were asked to retire. I was left alone in the hands of the doctor and his attendants. At his command I bared my back and sat down. The first stroke of his knife laid bare the length of my shoulder-blade, the next measured its breadth; then he dexterously cleft the flesh off the bone on each side, and getting a leverage under it raised it out of its place, and by the application of the saw took off several inches of the bone. It seemed like the cutting of red-hot instruments; but now I thought it was all over, and I stood it bravely.

"But after a little consultation the doctor said, 'Mr. Moody, you have extraordinary nerves. You stood that like a man; but I am sorry to tell you that, while I took off the protuberance entirely, I find that the disease has penetrated the bone much higher than I could have supposed, and it will be necessary in order to effect a permanent cure, to take off the bone as near to the shoulder as possible.'

"Thinking the worst was over my nerves had relaxed, and it cost me," said Moody, "a fearful struggle to get my courage up to the work; but I succeeded, and he cut away all the diseased bone. I became perfectly well, and as strong in that arm as in the other." "The word of God is quick and powerful, sharper than any two-edged sword, piercing even to the dividing asunder of soul and spirit and of the joints and marrow, and is a discerner of the thoughts and intents of the heart." The sinner must have such a desire to be saved, and such confidence in the Great Physician whom God hath sent to save the world, and hath so fully attested, and advertised in his Gospel, as to lay himself down on the surgical table of the Holy Spirit, and let him cut out right eye sins, and stand to it, and as certainly as the Lord liveth, he will be saved. This Great Physician never lost a case thus entrusted to his will.

But is this practical saving faith the result of the exercise of merely natural functions of faith?

Not by any means. *It is the Spirit* that giveth life. The eye can as readily see without a gleam of light as can natural faith apprehend and embrace

Jesus, apart from the direct revealing of the Holy Spirit. But the Holy Spirit adjusts his light and quickening influence to the laws of the human mind and moral constitution, and works through these natural powers in perfect harmony with the laws and processes of natural faith. As "the spirit of bondage to fear," he reveals to the sinner his lost condition and helplessness. Then comes the collision of the forces of light and darkness before described, and a variety of methods to obtain relief, till the flesh with its plans and hopes is crucified; meantime, the good Spirit teaches the seeking soul all things necessary from the Gospel, to which he assents, and submitting to God's will, he accepts Jesus Christ on the faith of God's testimony concerning him. The moment the Holy Spirit sees that a penitent thus submits, and in his heart believes—at the instance of God the Father, who justifieth in consideration of the merits and mediation of Jesus—he removes the burden of sin from his conscience, sheds the love of God abroad in his heart, and clearly attests the fact to his inner consciousness that his sins are all forgiven. "Being justified by faith he has peace with God through our Lord Jesus Christ." He now realizes *the end* and *demonstrative fruit* of believing, as thus stated by

St. Peter to St. Paul's churches in Asia Minor; referring to their "heaviness through manifold temptation, that the trial of your faith," says he, "being much more precious than gold that perisheth, though it be tried with fire, might be found unto praise, and honour, and glory at the appearing of Jesus Christ, whom having not seen ye love; in whom though now ye see him not, yet believing, ye rejoice with joy unspeakable and full of glory." Why? "Receiving the end of your faith"—the very thing for which ye believe—"even the salvation of your souls." Believing, then, is the act of receiving Christ on the faith of his Gospel credentials; and the demonstrative proof of the genuine character of my faith, and the effective degree of its exercise, is that I receive salvation, enabling me to rejoice with unspeakable joy. It is a ridiculous contradiction for a man to assume that he has saving faith, and remain in sin. The proof of the effectiveness of anything is in what it does. If a man is not saved from his sins, whatever else he may have, he has not saving faith, and the demonstration of it is in the fact that he is not saved.

But is not faith the gift of God?

Certainly. "By grace ye are saved"—not hope

to be saved—"through faith, and that not of yourselves, it is the gift of God. Not of works, lest any man should boast." The basis of faith, as before shown, is the gift of God; so with the object of faith—Jesus Christ; so with the natural functions; so of the quickening light and power of the Holy Spirit; so also the salvation we thus receive. We have no ground of boasting. These essential conditions to believing are all the gifts of God, but the exercise of faith is our act; as St. Paul says to his Gentile believers in the city of Ephesus, who had been gathered unto Christ, "In whom ye also trusted after that ye heard the word of truth, the gospel of your salvation: in whom also after that ye believed, ye were sealed with that Holy Spirit of promise."

Faith is not the gift of God in a sense that will preclude the necessity of proving ourselves whether we be in the faith, nor of searching the Scriptures to learn what we are to believe, and in accordance with the legitimate exercise of our natural functions of faith under the leading influence of the Holy Spirit, assent to God's facts, consent to his terms, and embrace Christ as a present Saviour, Nor is it a gift of God that will secure salvation without such an act of believing in the simple natural mode: nor, hence, is it the impartation of any new attribute of mind or heart, but an adjustment of gracious light and influence to our natural powers of mind and heart, and adequately exercised on our part; but in no sense coercively, so as to suspend the voluntary action of the soul in accepting or rejecting Christ. "He that believeth not is condemned already." Why? Because God did not give him faith, or all the essential conditions to believing? Nay! but "because he hath not believed in the name of the only begotten Son of God." Would God condemn any person for not doing what it was impossible for such a person to do? The very ground of condemnation is in the fact that God gave him every power essential to believing, and he refused to yield obedience, and exercise it. "This is the condemnation," the ground of condemnation, not that men have been sinners simply, "but that light is come into the world, and men love darkness rather than light, because their deeds were evil;" and hence walked after the flesh, and not after the Spirit. To the one, "faith is imputed to him for righteousness"—the only credit he has to his account in the matter is that, as a poor bankrupt ruined soul, "he accepted the free gift of God, which is eternal life through Jesus Christ." Nothing meritorious in that. The condemnation of the other is on the ground of his refusal to accept this gift "of eternal life." The condemnation is not so much an arbitrary punishment for the sin of rejecting Christ, though that is embraced, as in the fact of rejecting the only Saviour of sinners, and must, therefore, inevitably perish in default, and that without remedy. Hence, for a penitent to neglect the intelligent exercise of the natural functions requisite to believing, and the gracious ability imparted by the awakening spirit, and spend his time praying that God would give him faith, is not according to the Gospel, nor the philosophy of the facts in the case. St. Paul did not tell the Philippian jailer to pray for faith, but commanded him to "believe on the Lord Jesus Christ," to exercise the power of faith, natural and spiritual, that God had given to him, and which he gives to every sinner in Christendom. To pray "Lord increase our faith," is legitimate, for it is in harmony with one of God's great laws, that the right use of power tends to its increase. When the poor snake-bitten Israelites cried for help, "The Lord said unto Moses: Make thee a fiery serpent, and set it upon a pole; and it shall come to pass, that every one that is bitten, when he looketh upon it shall live." When the heralds ran through that vast encampment of probably two millions of souls, proclaiming God's remedy, and the condition on which the application depended, to refuse obedience on any pretext was fatal, to pray that God would give them eyes, would have been disobedience, with an insulting reflection on God, in commanding them to look in the absence of vision. "As Moses lifted up the serpent in the wilderness, even so" "the Son of Man" was "lifted up, that whosoever believeth in Him should not perish, but have everlasting life." The very command implies the certainty of God's adequate and available provision of all that is necessary to obedience.

But says one, "I try to believe and cannot; and must I not then pray that God would give me faith to believe?"

Nay; instead of assuming that the fault is with God in withholding the gifts necessary to obedience, admit the fact in the case, that the fault is with yourself, and honestly search for it, and ask God to give you increasing light—as he will, when you deal honestly with him—to see, and strength to remove the hindrances in yourself. This exercise of saving faith is so simple that it is very difficult to explain it to a seeker by abstract definitions. Any child understands what is meant by taking a drink of cold water, because it is a matter of experience; but if a man could be found who had no experience in such matters, and you should undertake to explain the simple process—the nature of thirst, the properties of water, the condition necessary to the application, the variety of mental, nervous, and muscular action employed in taking a drink of water—most likely the teacher and his pupil would be lost in a labyrinth of difficulties. Hence the necessity, in a matter involving your eternal life or death, of sticking to facts, and great principles, essential to right action. The Gospel supper is abundant and free, and the invitation has gone forth to a starving world, "Come, for all things are now ready." "Whosoever will let him take the water of life freely." "A pure river of water of life, clear as crystal, proceeding out of the throne of God and the lamb," wat ring and refreshing all heaven, and extending to the uttermost bounds of the earth.

"Its streams the whole creation reach,
So plenteous is the store;
Enough for all, enough for each,
Enough for evermore."

Repentance toward God, resulting in unreserved submission to his will, brings any poor sinner to the edge of this "river of water of life." Now, let us see how a plain thing is mystified by the traditions of men, that we may remove hindrances, and assist you in an intelligent acceptance of Christ as your Saviour.

Some teachers proclaim, "Repentance is not necessary; only believe and you will be saved." That is equivalent to saying to a famishing man, half a mile away from the river's brink, no need to go to the river, just drink where you are.

Others say to the thirsting, dying multitude, "Struggle on, pray on, you'll get relief when you die. If you drink of the river of water of life you can never know the fact, nor feel any certain relief for your burning thirst till your dying day."

Here comes a famishing sinner. Now he is at the brink of the river, but he is blind, and wants some kind friend to help him to get his burning lips to its cooling surface. Up comes a learned doctor, and says to the poor fellow, "My friend, which way did you come?"

"I can hardly tell," replies the poor soul. "I had an awful time in getting here. I could not see my way; but I believe I came right over fences, hedges, and ditches. I thought if I could only get here it would be all right, no matter by which route I came; for I could hear the roar of the river, and a kind voice, saying, 'Come and take freely.'"

The doctor replies gravely, "My dear friend, you did not come by the right path. You must go back," and then went on to say, "at such a cross-road turn to the right, further along turn to the left, then at a certain point turn to the right again." The directions were so complicated that they could not be remembered. But the poor soul was sent back, to find the way as best he could. Poor fellow, after the struggle of years he may blunder back to the river, but is more likely to famish and die in the desert of unbelief.

Here comes another, with groaning and tears, covered with dust and perspiration, crying, "Men and brethren, what shall I do?"

A grave-looking man approaches him, saying, "Excuse me, stranger, but I want to warn you against presumption." "O sir, I'm dying with thirst, can't I get down to this river and drink?" "You should remember that you have been a hardened rebel for many years."

"O yes, I confess it all. I have consented to give up all my wicked ways, but need strength for the new life I want to lead."

"Yes, but after so many years of sin, it is too much for you to expect to be allowed to drink as much as you want at once. You should keep back, and fast and pray, and show to the world the sincerity of your repentance, and the soundness of your reformation, and then you may find a place at which you may drink."

"O my dear sir, I have been fasting, and praying, and struggling to get to the river; I can do nothing myself, unless I get strength by drinking the water of life. O lead me down to the brink, that I may drink and live."

"You must not be in haste in this grave matter, sir. Impatience is a great sin. You must wait God's own time."

There stands a poor man shivering on the brink.

"My dear friend, get down on your knees there, like Gideon's humble warriors, and drink."

"O, I'm not at the right place."

"You are on the river's edge, and you have only to get down and drink."

"But, O dear sir, I am such a dreadful sinner,

I am not worthy to put my polluted lips to the waters of life."

"True, but this 'fountain was opened for sin and uncleanness;' and all sinners are invited to come and drink freely."

"Oh! dear me, I do feel so badly. I wish I could get relief."

"Drink, and you will get relief in a moment."

"O I am in an awful state; will God ever have mercy on such a sinner?"

"Why, my dear sir, he has had mercy on you. He provided the river for all such as you. He sent his Spirit into the desert after you, and hath led you now to this exhaustless supply, and invites you to take freely. Now drink, or you will perish. There is no possibility of relief except by drinking."

"Oh! I cannot drink. O that God would give me power to drink."

"I beseech you, if you value your soul, don't try to ignore God's great facts, brought within demonstrable range of your own experience. Honestly admit God's facts, revealing your need, and this abundant supply. Thankfully accept God's offer. God would not command you to drink, and withhold the power to do so. You do not know what you can do till truthfully you say,

> 'I will accept his offers now,
> From every sin depart.'

and drink till your burning thirst is alleviated, and your soul is healed. The only possible bar is your refusal to drink; the only limit, that of your capacity. You might as well try to drink the Amazon or St. Lawrence dry, as this river of life. All the world may drink, and not cause the ebb of one figure below the grand high-water gauge of God's immutable purpose to save the world." The poor fellow drinks, and is saved, and blushes in astonishment that, through the most unreasonable and God-dishonouring unbelief, he had shivered on the brink so long.

CHAPTER VII.

SAVING EXERCISE OF FAITH.

Now, my dear friend, to pass from this hypothetical mode of illustrating this important subject, I will give you in more direct forms some of the popular modes of instruction to seeking sinners, and then explain and illustrate what I conceive to be the more excellent way.

I have often heard persons say to a penitent, "Believe that you have pardon, and you will have it." That involves a double absurdity: to beiieve what the sinner knows is not true—a falsehood—and then receive what he assumed to be in possession of before he believed.

I heard a man of repute for intelligence and piety, say to a seeker of pardon: "God pardoned you, my dear sir, before you were born, and you must believe that fact and praise him."

If he meant God's provision of pardon for him

and for the world, he should have said so; but the fact of his personal forgiveness was conditioned on his own act of believing, and could not precede it.

I heard another say, "If you can only believe that Jesus died for sinners, and that you are a sinner, you are saved."

I consider that an injudicious jumbling of truth, that may in some cases help, but is more likely to hinder the seeking soul.

Some say, "Believe that God receives you now, and he will."

But suppose he does not, in fact, receive the said sinner at that moment, then he is asked to believe what is not true. If a soul is actually embracing Christ by faith, such advice might help him, as the true light sometimes shines through erroneous forms of truth, but it does not define what a penitent is to believe.

The exercise of saving faith is a rational, intelligible thing, and it is a great pity that it should be the subject of so much loose definition and random application. It is not, to be sure, a mere exercise of reason, but like all God's perceivable arrangements commends itself to reason, and though much higher in its sphere and ends, is not opposed to reason.

When I undertake to work together with the Holy Spirit in leading a soul to Christ—and it has been my daily business for upwards of twenty-five years of my life—I enquire first into the spiritual condition of the seeker by such questions as these: "Have you ever known the Lord in the pardon of your sins? Have you been seeking him a long, or short period? Hath the good Spirit so given you to see the 'exceeding sinfulness of sin,' not only in its consequences to yourself, but its heinousness in the sight of God, as to lead you to abhor and renounce it? You not only desire to give up sin, but have you developed that desire into a fact? "Do you now consent to a divorce from all sin—sins of the heart and of the life—right eye and right hand sins—not to save yourself, you cannot—but consent that God destroy all your idols, and 'separate your sins from you, as far as the east is from the west,' and accept his will as the rule of your heart and life? If you seek as a mere experiment you will not succeed. There must be an honest confession of your sins, and your helplessness, and an unreserved consecration of your whole being to God, for time and for eternity. If you now consent thus to submit yourself to God's will you have but to believe, and you will be saved."

What are you to believe?

Not that you are pardoned, for you know you are not.

Not that you can do some saving penitential work to commend you to God's favour. If you could shed a river of tears, "give all your goods to feed the poor, and your body to be burned," you could not atone for one sin. There is but one "sacrifice for sins." The end, or object, of your repentance is unreserved submission to God's will.

Not that you are to obtain relief first, from your dreadful hardness and darkness, and the repellant forces of sin and Satan, and then believe; nay, relief can only be had by the saving power of Jesus, and believing is the condition. If you were suffering an attack of cholera, you would not say, "As soon as I can get relief from these dreadful pains and cramps, then I will give my case into the hands of a physician." So you must give your case into the hands of your great Physician just as you are. Come with all your hardness, and darkness; your guilt and bondage, wretched and ruined by sin; utterly helpless, and hopeless in yourself, trusting to nothing you have done, or can do, or that anybody else can do for you; just as you are, give your case into the hands of Jesus, and believe.

Believe what? "Believe the Gospel." "Believe the record of God concerning his Son." God hath found a ransom, provided a remedy, proclaimed an almighty Saviour, and hath told us in his gospel all that is necessary to command our faith in him; and you must believe what he says. A Saviour that God hath provided, accepted, and proclaimed, is every way worthy of our confidence.

What, simply assent to these facts?

Nay, the devils do that much; but assenting, you must accept Jesus Christ as your Saviour, on the faith of those facts. "It is a faithful saying, and worthy to be accepted" by all, "that Christ Jesus came into the world to save sinners," even the "chief of sinners." That is the declared object of his great mission. Is he not competent? Now, on the faith of God's facts and recommendations, you must repose confidence in Jesus, and accept him as your Saviour—confidence in his blood-shedding on the cross as an adequate sacrifice for the sins of the whole world, and hence for your sins, constituting the meritorious ground for the removal of all the legal difficulties involved in your antagonism to the immutable principles of righteousness in God's moral government, and the procuring ground of "pardon, holiness, and heaven;" confidence in his prayers as your great High Priest, "who was delivered for our offences, and raised again for our justification." "Who will have all men to be saved, and to come unto the knowledge of the truth; For there is one God, and one mediator between God and man, the man Christ Jesus, who gave himself a ransom for all, to be testified in due time." God testified his acceptance of the ransom in that "he raised him from the dead, and set him at his own right hand in heavenly places;" and Jesus in his mediation testifies to the adequacy of his redeeming acts. Can you not entrust your cause in the hands of such an advocate with the Father in heaven's court? Confidence in his invitations and promises. "Come unto me, all ye that labour and are heavy laden, and I will give you rest. Take my yoke upon you, and learn of me, for I am meek and lowly of heart; and ye shall find rest unto your souls." He is meek and lowly of heart, more kind, sympathising, and approachable than any human friend in the world. Can't you trust him? Confidence in his ability to save you. The Jewish priests were weak as reeds shaken with the wind, and "were not suffered to continue by reason of death; but this man, because he continueth ever, hath an unchangeable priesthood. Wherefore he is able to save them to the uttermost that come unto God by him"—save effectively from the uttermost depths of degradation: save all of every clime and nation that come unto God by him; save to the uttermost limit of time till he shall deliver up his mediatorial kingdom, and sit in judgment upon the world—"seeing he ever liveth to make intercession for them." Can you doubt his ability to save you now. Confidence in his willingness to save you. "Christ hath loved us, and hath given himself for us, an offering and a sacrifice to God"—"hath poured out his soul unto death" for us. He is the only friend you have, who loves you enough to die for you. He loves you more than your mother ever did, or ever could. His great heart of sympathy, remember, is the same now, precisely, as when he poured ou his heart's blood on Calvary to redeem you. There is "no variableness or shadow of turning" in him. No "yea and nay" in him, "for all the promises of God in him, are yea, and in him amen." "Jesus Christ, the same yesterday, and to-day, and for ever." What a mercy that we have such a friend in heaven's court! Oh! thankfully and gladly entrust all your interests of soul and body for time and for eternity in his care. Remember, too, my dear friend, that he is just as available now as he was to the poor lepers and blind men who came to him when manifest in the flesh. "Say not in thine heart, who shall ascend into heaven? that is, to bring Christ down from above. Or, who shall descend into the deep? that is to bring Christ again from the dead. But what saith it?" What saith God's immutable oracle on the subject? "The word is nigh thee, even in thy mouth, and in thy heart: that is, the word of faith which we preach"—"The record of God concerning his Son"—the basis of your faith in Christ—is so impressed on your heart, and so defined in speakable terms to your mouth, by the Holy Spirit, as to enforce upon you the responsibility of a decision now. You must confess and accept Christ as your Saviour now, or deny and reject him. You cannot improve your own state by delay; you cannot substitute something else for God's only Saviour of men; you cannot subsidize his atoning provision. It is all complete, perfect, and available now, and all in the person of the risen living Jesus, who is now "knocking at the door;" neither is there salvation in any other: "for there is none other name under heaven given among men, whereby we must be saved." "To him give all the prophets witness, that through his name whosoever believeth in him shall receive remission of sin." A postponement of your believing now, is a refusal. O my dear friend, do accept the glorious alternative just now.

The moment you thus submit to God's will, and thus in your heart intelligently believe in the Lord Jesus Christ—and accept him as your Saviour—that moment "God who justifieth" at the instance of your Mediator, will say, "Your sins are forgiven you for his name's sake;" and God the Holy Ghost will fulfil in your heart "the righteousness of the law;"—certify by the stamp of his royal seal upon your heart that the death-penalty of the law against you is cancelled, your sins forgiven, your right relation to God and his laws secured, and the love of God—the essential principle of obedience—shed abroad in your heart by the Holy Ghost thus given unto you; and all attested by the Spirit's direct witness, corroborated by the testimony of your own spirit, based on the conscious work and fruits of God's Holy Spirit in your experience. "Hereby know we that we dwell in him, and he in us, because he hath given us of his Spirit." "After that ye believed, ye were sealed with the Holy Spirit of promise, which is the earnest of our inheritance."

"The spirit of bondage to fear" hath now become "the spirit of adoption, whereby we cry, Abba, Father. The Spirit itself beareth witness with our spirits that we are the children of God. And, if children, then heirs; heirs of God, and joint heirs with Christ: if so be that we suffer with him, that we may also be glorified together." "Being justified by faith, we have peace with God, through our Lord Jesus Christ." The peace follows the pardon, and the pardon follows the believing; God's act of pardoning a believing penitent is called justification, no doubt because it is essentially a judicial act—an act of divine clemency, but in strict accordance with the highest principles of immutable justice, through the compensative provision of redemption.

By a decision of heaven's court, changing my relation from a condemned criminal to an adopted child, my relationship to God and his laws, which had been so sadly disjointed by sin, is adjusted.

The justification by works, of which St. James speaks, is the maintenance of this right adjustment of our relationships to God and his laws, by a continuous, living, developing faith, working by love, purifying the heart, and manifesting itself appropriately in word and deed. By faith we are engrafted into the true vine, by faith we abide in the true vine, but we thus daily derive the divine sap through the purifying life of the Holy Spirit, which manifests itself in the fruits of holiness.

Every principle and fact essential to this glorious adjustment, called justification, in the first place, must be maintained, developed, and suitably manifested, otherwise disjointment and death, instead of justification, will follow. "Shall we sin because we are not under the law, but under grace? God forbid. Know ye not that to whom ye yield yourselves servants to obey, his servants ye are to whom ye obey"—or yield obedience—"whether of sin unto death or of obedience unto righteousness."

Observe, those warning words were addressed to believers. The poor soul who presumes that, having obtained pardon, he may now tamper with unrighteousness in heart or life, and hold God to an unconditional covenant to maintain his heirship, outrages the instincts of common sense, the plain teachings of the whole Bible on the subject, and becomes a servant of sin unto death. "Whosoever is born of God doth not commit sin, for his seed remaineth in him"—this new life imparted or planted in his heart by the Holy Spirit—"and he cannot sin because he is born of God." St. John does not teach the impossibility, for in the same letter he admits the possibility, and the fact, and all through solemnly warns believers of the danger of their falling into sin, but teaches emphatically, what all the other apostles taught, that sin was of the devil, and hence entirely incongruous with their new life, and relations, as children of God, and hence utterly inadmissible—they cannot remain children of God and commit sin. So when St. Paul was expatiating on our glorious heirship with Jesus Christ, he was careful to add this essential condition, that which runs on till we the crown obtain—"If so be that we suffer with him that we may be also glorified together." The doctrine of St. Paul and St. James, on justification by faith as the ground or condition, and by works as legitimate fruit and demonstration of faith, is clearly stated by St. Paul, thus :—"For we ourselves also were sometimes foolish, disobedient, deceived, serving divers lusts and pleasures, living in malice and envy, hateful and hating one another. But after that the kindness and love of God our Saviour toward man appeared, not by works of righteousness which we have done, but according to his mercy he saved us, by the washing of regeneration, and renewing of the Holy Ghost, which he shed on us abundantly through Jesus Christ our Saviour; that being justified by his grace, we should be made heirs according to the hope of eternal life. This is a faithful saying, and these things I will that thou"—Titus, and all ministers of the Gospel—"affirm constantly that they which have believed in God might be careful to maintain good works. These are good and profitable unto men." The assumption that the apostles taught a contradictory doctrine is full of the insidious poison of infidelity. If such is the fact, then they were not inspired, and hence their teachings are not authoritative, or if inspired, then God contradicted himself, and hence we have no reliable basis of faith in him. But it is clearly in evidence, that the assumption is false, and that God's oracles, all in beautiful harmony, teach the same great doctrines, and the more closely we investigate the subject under the Holy Spirit's teaching light the more clearly we see this fact.

Now, my dear friend, having defined briefly some of the legitimate fruits, and relative bearings of faith, we will return to the leading thread of our discourse, and explain and illustrate a little more fully this essential condition of salvation—believing.

"Suppose," says one of my friends, "after I submit to God's will, assent to God's facts, and on the faith of those facts accept Jesus Christ as my Saviour, I do not receive the regenerating work and witness of the Spirit."

My dear friend, that is not a supposable case. All God's provisions are immutable verities. The renewing work and witness of the Spirit in the hearts of all believers are as much a matter of provision as the blood-shedding itself, and as immutably reliable. As well may a man talk about drinking from the flowing river without wetting his lips, or feeling the cooling, refreshing effect. Some, to be sure, acquire such a habit of doubting God's facts, that when they do submit, and in the desperation of despair cling to Jesus, they will not credit the Spirit's work and testimony within their own hearts, and hence for a time linger in darkness, and emerge into the light so gradually that they cannot tell the precise hour nor day when they obtained "remission of sins;" and others go on doubting to their dying day. But neither of these is according to God's purpose and provision.

It is, however, not uncommon for persons to say, "I do submit, and I do believe, but I can't get any relief." Such persons simply mistake their own assumptions for facts.

At a meeting in Sidney one night of a series of services, where some hundreds of souls believed and were saved, a brother said to me, "That lady has had a hard struggle, but she has come through all right. She is believing, and I think she is happy."

Approaching her gently, I said, "My sister, have you surrendered yourself unreservedly to God?"

"O yes, I do give up everything—to be or to do whatever is his will."

"Are you believing in Jesus?" I had before explained to her the way of salvation by faith.

"O yes, I do believe in Jesus. I do accept him as my Saviour."

"Do you realize peace with God through believing?"

"No, sir, I am sorry to say I experience no comfort whatever."

"Now, my dear sister, allow me to say, I cannot see your heart, and you may not see it yet as you ought; but God the Holy Spirit, who is leading you to seek Jesus, sees it just as it is; and I tell you, that the very moment he sees that from your heart you do submit fully to God's will, and do in your heart accept Jesus Christ as your Saviour, that very moment he will remove the burden of guilt from your conscience, shed the sweet forgiving love of God abroad in your heart, and assure you of the fact that being justified by faith you have peace with God. There is either a defect in your submission, or in your believing, or in both. Now, honestly search your heart, and I will meantime pray the good Spirit to give you increasing light, and you will soon find out the hindrance; and if you consent to its removal, you will believe, 'and receive the end of your faith, even the salvation of your soul.'" She evidently went into a close heart examination. For a few moments she wept as though her heart-strings were breaking, and, in fact, "repented and believed the Gospel," and was filled "with joy unspeakable and full of glory" in less than ten minutes from the commencement of the interview just given. The Holy Spirit alone is competent to decide when a poor sinner submits and believes; and the proof of the actual fact of such surrender and believing is in the "demonstration of the Spirit," through his regenerating and witnessing work in the heart; which, to be sure, must be subsequent to the act of believing, but is, nevertheless, the demonstrated fact that the penitent is believing."

"The traditions of men," and the ingenious negatives of Satan in the form of "ifs, buts, and cant's," constitute a serious embarrassment to seekers.

Passing round among the seekers in York-street, Sydney, one night, I approached a seeker and explained to him in simplicity how to be saved by faith in Jesus.

After listening attentively till I had done, he promptly replied, "I am a Scotchman, sir. I can't get into it by any such short method as that. It will take me a long time to work my way in."

"Yes, sir, if it depended on your works, you might struggle on till the day of your death, and would never get into the kingdom at all. But if you must be saved, "not by works of righteousness but by the mercy of God," in virtue of the perfected atonement and gracious provision of Jesus, why not now? God can save a Scotchman as quickly as he can save an Irishman, or any other name or form of man in the world. He will save no man while he refuses to yield obedience, and rejects Christ, but will save any and every man the very moment they do submit and believe."

Then he commenced to pray again with increasing earnestness, pleading that God would come and have mercy on him. I saw that he was still in the dark on the essential duty of believing, and got his attention again by saying, "Now, my dear brother, I believe, as you say, that under the Spirit's awakening you do consent to a divorce from all sin, and to accept God's will as the rule of your life; but you are looking for God to do some wonderful thing for you, and then accept you, while God is looking for you to recognize and thankfully appreciate the wonderful thing he hath done for you, and for every poor sinner, through the atonement of Christ, and accept him. The Spirit's renewing work, which will certainly follow, is a part of his immutable purpose and provision, and you need give yourself no trouble on that subject. The Spirit of adoption will attend to that. Your duty is to 'repent and believe the Gospel,' and to do it now." He received some light, but was not saved till the next night.

Some months afterwards, in a fellowship meeting,

referring to the night he found peace with God. I heard him say, "I felt sin a grievous burden pressing upon my soul. The Spirit of God said to my heart, 'Bow down at that altar of prayer; confess your sins, and accept Christ now.' Satan said to my heart, 'Go home, and read your Bible, and meditate and pray alone.' Thank God, I was enabled to detect the subtle snare of Satan, and resisted him. I bowed down there, surrendered my wicked heart to God, believed in the Lord Jesus Christ, and found salvation. I have been happy in the enjoyment of the precious love of Jesus in my heart ever since."

Satan's most destructive weapons are often concealed under the most plausible forms of truth and pious performances. To "go home and meditate, read the Bible, and pray," were certainly all appropriate enough in their place, but when the good Spirit has led a soul to the very edge of the river of life, and commands him now "to take the water of life freely;" to believe now "in the Lord Jesus Christ"—then to substitute anything whatsoever for a present acceptance of a present Saviour, is a deceitful snare of Satan leading to that most dreadful sin which peoples hell—unbelief.

At the close of a meeting one night in Auckland,

New Zealand, a shipmaster came forward, and expressing his desire for a short interview. said to me, "I heard you preach in Hobart Town last year, and I have felt very miserable ever since. I have been attending your preaching here, and have made up my mind, by the help of God, to lead a different life."

I questioned him closely, and found him to be under the awakening power of the Spirit to a degree that would lead him to a surrender to God, and I said to him, "Captain, I am very glad that God hath sent his Spirit to show you your sinful state and danger. God is very kind. He hath 'nourished and brought you up,' and though you have rebelled against him so long and so grievously, he hath borne patiently with you. Jesus hath continued to intercede for you, and hath now sent his good Spirit to call you, and lead you to him, that you may find rest for your soul. The very fact that you thus feel the influence of his convincing Spirit is proof that he loves you, and is very desirous to save you. But, Captain, allow me to tell you that Satan has laid a fatal snare for you, and you are proposing to yourself to go right into it by your plausible plan for a reformation. You say you are determined to lead a new life, but how can you lead a new life without a new heart; 'The Ethiopian cannot change his skin, nor the leopard his spots.' Your very nature, as you feel and confess, is corrupt, and full of enmity against God; you are a prisoner of the Divine law, under sentence of death, and it will be time for you to talk about fulfilling the duties of citizenship in 'the commonwealth of Israel' when you are released from the death-sentence, and become a 'fellow-citizen with the saints, and of the household of God.' Moreover you are in the most abject bondage to sin and Satan, as is proven in your own experience by the thousands of good resolutions you have broken before. Your only hope of deliverance is to confess all these facts to God, surrender your helpless soul to him, and accept Jesus Christ, whom he hath sent to seek and to save the lost. If you cannot submit now under the gracious influences which you feel, what can you hope to do when you get back into the old slippery paths of business and worldly associations? Do you not see that you would relapse into the same dead state; nay be more dead even than before, by having grieved the Holy Spirit in rejecting his offers of salvation. If you 'now confess and forsake your sins,' and accept God's perfected remedy in Christ, you will obtain pardon to-night. The Spirit of adoption will give you a new heart, and then under his leading you will live the life for God you are proposing to yourself."

"O," said he, "I am in a dreadful state, but I am not ready to receive pardon to-night."

"But, my dear sir, you will never make yourself any better. Do you now consent that God shall remove all your idols and sins, and utterly consume them, and conform your heart and life to his own will?"

"O yes, I am very anxious, but I must learn to pray."

"Now, my dear brother, that is just another form of the same old thing. Satan will lead you to reject Christ, and get you to substitute some plan of your own, if you let him. 'Learn to pray!' How long did it require the poor publican, when he felt the crushing weight of his sins upon him, as you do to-night, to learn to cry, 'God be merciful to me a sinner?' Prayer is telling God the burden and desire of your heart, as you have told me.' 'The spirit of bondage to fear' is working in you now to 'will and to do,' and your heart is full of the subject matter for prayer, and you have only to open your mouth, and God will graciously help you to pray. Submit and believe, and believing, you will receive the end of your faith, even the salvation of your soul."

With that, he dropped on his knees, and cried earnestly to God for mercy, and in less than a quarter of an hour he accepted Jesus as his present Saviour, and was filled with joy and gladness, and went to his ship praising God for salvation by faith.

When I was labouring in Mudgee, New South Wales, a man who had been forward as a seeker several times, was crying out, "I can't believe! Oh! I can't believe!"

Said I, "My friend, you must believe, or you will perish." I had previously satisfied myself as to the sincerity and depth of his repentance.

"But," replied he, "I can't believe. I've tried again and again, and I can't, I know I can't believe."

"That is the essence of unbelief—the very plague-spot of perdition. It is a wicked reflection on God to say you cannot do what God commands. Would God require you, under the penalty of eternal death, to do what he had not put within your power? you should be very careful how you charge God with such an outrageous procedure as all that: God hath given you all the natural functions necessary to believing—hath furnished in the Bible the most reliable basis of faith in the world, hath sent his quickening Spirit to impart all the Divine stimulus necessary to believing, and is waiting to reveal Jesus Christ the almighty Saviour of sinners to your heart, the very moment you consent to his terms."

"But," said he, "I must tell the truth. What is the use of my saying I can believe when I feel I can't? What shall I say?"

"Well, sir, instead of telling God that you have no confidence in what he says, and cannot accept his provision of mercy, approach him in simplicity, as did the poor lepers and blind men we read about in the Gospel, and say, 'O God, thou seest me. Thou knowest what a polluted sinner I am. Thou knowest the hardness of my heart, the blindness of my mind, and my utter inability to make myself any better. Thou knowest that I am under the death sentence of thy law, and in bondage to sin and Satan, and in myself utterly helpless, and hopeless, and all the good men and angels in the universe, combined, could not save me from my sins and their consequences. But, O God, I have read in thy book that thou hast found a ransom, provided a remedy, proclaimed an almighty

Saviour 'able to save to the uttermost all that come unto God by him.' O God, I dare not contradict thy statements. Thy servant, St. John, hath said, 'He that believeth on the Son of God hath the witness in himself; he that believeth not God hath made him a liar, because he believeth not the record that God gave of his Son, and this is the record'—the substance and end of it—'that God hath given to us eternal life, and this life is in his Son.' This free gift of God—salvation from sin and eternal life—is not in any work of our own, past or future, not in any detached portion of Christ's redeeming work, not even in the blood of the cross, but all the saving virtue of the whole work of redemption, and the divine power for its application, are embodied in the person of the risen Jesus. 'He that hath the Son hath life, and he that hath not the Son hath not life.' If, my dear brother, on the faith of God's most reliable record, you accept Christ as your Saviour, in him you will find pardon and life. But instead of that you are telling God you cannot believe what he says about Jesus, and hence, cannot accept him as your Saviour. My dear sir, do not in addition to your life of rebellion against God, now that he hath kindly sent his Spirit to lead you to Jesus, call him a liar, and reject his Son, but tell him that you cannot doubt the truth of his record concerning his Son, and that you will give your poor soul into his hands."

"O God, have mercy on me, and forgive my wicked unbelief," cried he. "I never will again say, I can't believe; I will try."

Leaving him to his reflections for a season, I afterwards returned and said—"Well, my brother, how do you get on?"

"Oh! I cannot believe! What made me say that, I did not mean to say that any more."

"Ah, Satan, is playing on your old habits of unbelief, and helping you in that matter, but you must at once and for ever strike the words 'I can't believe' out of your spiritual vocabulary."

"If the Lord will help me, and I believe he will," said he, "I will never say it again." The meeting for that night was at that juncture brought to a close, and he retired without salvation, but was "looking to Jesus." Early next morning he came o tell me that he had accepted Jesus, and in him had found life and salvation. He was weeping tears of joy, and praising God; frequently expressing meantime, his great astonishment, that, during four years of earnest seeking, he had groped in the darkness of such God-dishonouring unbelief. Many months afterwards I learned that he was living "by faith," and walking "in the light."

Now my friend, I have sufficiently illustrated the grounds of faith. Its OBJECT. Its natural functions. Its spiritual vitality. Its simple exercise, and its experimental demonstrative fruits. The illustrative examples I have given you are by no means peculiar or exceptional, unless it be in mere verbal expression, but they are simply specimen examples of the common experience of millions of believers, in exact accordance with the plain teachings of the Bible.

God is reconciled to the whole world on the conditions of the gospel treaty, and all the resources and agencies of the gospel are employed to persuade a world of perishing rebels to be reconciled to God, "All things"—necessary to our salvation—"are of God, who hath reconciled us"—all believers—"to himself by Jesus Christ, and hath given to us the ministry of reconciliation. To wit, that God was in Christ reconciling the world unto himself, not imputing their trespasses unto them."—Not reconciling himself to the world, he is reconciled to the world conditionally, and as soon as any of them sign the treaty—"set to their seal that God is true," then they become, effectively, parties to the covenant of mercy, recipients of its pardon, and heirs to all its glorious provisions.—" And hath committed unto us"—the ambassadors of Christ, and his Church, embracing all true believers—" the word of reconciliation." " Now then we are ambassadors for Christ as though God did beseech you by us, we pray you in Christ's stead, be ye reconciled to God." What a pity, that after all, so many sinners persistently refuse to " acquaint themselves with God, and be at peace," and receive the offered gift of eternal life.

My friend, " do ye now believe?" When the facts of the case are brought clearly before you, delay is out of the question.

Some months ago, in company with a party of dear friends, I was going to cross the Auckland Bay to visit " the lake." Mr. S———, a gentleman of fortune, came to see us off. I said to him, " Come with us, brother S———, we have plenty of room for you, and shall be glad to have the pleasure of your company."

" Thank you," replied he, " I would be happy to accompany you, but I have an engagement that demands my attention to-day."

" Surely a gentleman of leisure, who has retired

from business, can spare a few hours on recreation and health account."

"No; to tell you the truth about it, my insurance policy ran out to-day, and I must go at once, and have it renewed before the office closes."

I then played on the unreasonable procrastinating habits of sinners, by assuming to beg him to risk his property till to-morrow, and seek his pastime pleasure to-day, but he broke it off abruptly, saying, "Excuse me, I must hasten before the office closes."

"Who among us shall dwell with the devouring fire? Who among us shall dwell with everlasting burnings?" My friend, is your soul insured against those everlasting burnings? If not, don't risk it till to-morrow.

"God hath prepared thee a home,
Sinner, canst thou believe it?
He now invites thee come,
Sinner, wilt thou receive it?

"O come, sinner, come,
For the tide is receding,
And Jesus will soon
And for ever cease pleading."

THE END.

www.ingramcontent.com/pod-product-compliance
Lightning Source LLC
LaVergne TN
LVHW011207110826
845150LV00006B/1355